HOME AGAIN

HOME AGAIN

A Prayerful Rediscovery
of Your Catholic Faith

Fr. John Henry Hanson, O. Praem.

Scepter

Published by Scepter Publishers, Inc.

info@scepterpublishers.org

www.scepterpublishers.org

800-322-8773

New York

All rights reserved.

Cover art: Rembrandt Harmensz van Rijn, The Visitation, 1640. The Picture Art Collection / Alamy Stock Photo

Cover design: by Studio Red Design

Text design and pagination: by Studio Red Design

Library of Congress Control Number: 2019957377

ISBN

Paperback: 9781594173714

eBook: 9781594173721

Printed in the United States of America

TABLE OF CONTENTS

INTRODUCTION
What Roads Were Meant For

Cannot you be grateful for the road though it be rough and uncertain? It does all a road was ever meant to do. It takes you home.

—FATHER BEDE JARRETT, OP[1]

I f you've reached the age when you've begun holding small print (or small items in general) away from yourself to see them better, the following analogy will make special sense to you. If you're among those whose vision requires the opposite movement, close up instead of at arm's length, a parallel analogy can be made; and it will be made in due time. Spiritually, both near and farsightedness are necessary; each, in fact, demands the other. They form two optics by which we must see the most important things.

The comparison is drawn from the first pages of G. K. Chesterton's

---

1   Bede Jarrett, OP, *No Abiding City*, (London: Burns, Oates & Washbourne, 1938). P. 30-31, 32

classic *The Everlasting Man*. Chesterton sketches an intriguing image of a young man leaving home on some undefined quest: to find some colossal monument, some grand thing that could never be found within the tame confines of home and village. But once he has traveled a significant distance, turning to give the homestead a second look, he finds his familiar home quite different from what he thought it was while he was actually there—more magnificent and exciting than he could appreciate close-up. Sometimes, Chesterton suggests, the greatness of something is underappreciated if not missed altogether because it is "too large and too close to be seen."[2]

These reflections are written as a meditative guidebook for those willing to pause and look back, a few moments at a time, at that place St. Paul calls "the household of faith" (Gal 6:10). Revisiting the familiar territory of our faith, reacquainting ourselves with the persons and events that furnish the content and environment of our faith and its mysteries, is the itinerary proposed. The itinerary or program, in other words, is that of evangelization, old or new.

St. John Paul II assured us at the turn of the millennium that in order to gain a "new impetus for Christian living" there is no need to innovate:

> It is not therefore a matter of inventing a "new program." The program already exists: it is the plan found in the Gospel and in the living Tradition, it is the same as ever. Ultimately, it

---

2   G. K. Chesterton, *The Everlasting Man* (New York: Dodd, Mead & Company, 1925), Introduction, p. xi.

has its center in Christ himself, who is to be known, loved and imitated, so that in him we may live the life of the Trinity.... This is a program which does not change with shifts of times and cultures....[3]

But for this changeless program to work, as for the reflections in this book to bear fruit, prayerful contemplation is a must. The same holy pope tells us that "it would be wrong to think that ordinary Christians can be content with a shallow prayer that is unable to fill their whole life." Trying to face today's world without a deep prayer life renders Christians not only "mediocre," but puts them "at risk."[4]

The Prodigal Son easily comes to mind as the Biblical figure "at risk" par excellence: the young man who distances himself from the family home only to find that, at a remove of many miles, his father's house appears much more welcoming than when he had actually lived under its roof. He had thought he knew the best home had to offer; he thought he had exhausted all of his options there. But deep reflection proved him wrong. Never mind that his contemplation took place over a pigsty in a foreign country. The fact remains: Only by contemplatively comparing his past and present did he begin to see the reality of his life. The people and setting most familiar to him had become new again.

In the same way, you are not likely meet anyone you haven't met

3   John Paul II, Apostolic Letter at the Close of the Great Jubilee of the Year 2000, *Novo Millennio Ineunte* (January 6, 2001), 29.

4   *Novo Millennio*, 34.

or at least heard of before in these pages. Nor are you likely to be surprised by the events recounted. It is rather our willingness to see old things anew that will make the difference. The "same old thing" can look quite new when the beholder makes a point of circling around it and asking why it's shaped and colored that way, and even how it got there to begin with.

Why God chose a manger for his first bed, for instance, or a fishing boat to teach from, a donkey for a royal procession, and a wooden cross to die on, are not details we can dismiss as the familiar plot devices of childhood stories. God actually (and *eternally*) chose these things to make a point to us. We need to think about and pray over them. That he doesn't always explain them to us is no defect or oversight on his part. God expects us to study these things, but especially to *contemplate* them prayerfully. This is the one work that is never done, neither in time nor in eternity.

If the *Catechism of the Catholic Church* indicates this contemplation as the source of our supreme happiness in heaven, then what delight should it afford for us in this world?

> Because of his transcendence, God cannot be seen as he is, unless he himself opens up his mystery to man's immediate contemplation and gives him the capacity for it. The Church calls this contemplation of God in his heavenly glory "the beatific vision." (*CCC* 1028)

> The beatific vision, in which God opens himself in an inexhaustible way to the elect, will be the ever-flowing well-

spring of happiness, peace, and mutual communion. (*CCC* 1045)

No doubt our contemplation in this world limps—fraught, as it is, with pressures and distractions that take the mind far afield from the highest things. St. Paul confirms the obscurity of our prayer in describing it as seeing dimly in a mirror, as understanding the Lord only in a fragmentary way, while raising our hopes to seeing him "face to face" when we finally (and fully) understand "even as I have been fully understood" (See: 1 Cor 13:12).

But the basic trajectory remains the same: God opening himself in an inexhaustible way as contemplation unfolds, drawing us out of ourselves and into himself. This dynamic is what keeps monks and nuns rooted in their cloisters, priests enraptured at the altar, and all souls of prayer on the lookout for moments of quiet with the Lord.

The Lord blesses and repays our efforts in the trenches of prayer by gifting us with deeper knowledge and love of himself, so as to prepare us for what our eyes have never seen, our ears heard, nor our hearts conceived (See: 1 Cor 2:9). As in any love relationship, closeness to the other by knowledge and affection is what makes true union possible. So that the more we strive to enter into the mystery of God's saving love via contemplation, the deeper we travel into the core of the divine heart that loves us. In other words, we get closer to the source of the "ever-flowing well-spring of happiness, peace, and mutual communion." In a profound way, we can direct the words of the psalmist to the heart of God: "All my springs are in you" (Ps 87:7).

If there is nothing new to say about, or add to, the deposit of the

Christian faith, the Bible yet affirms the perennial newness of God's self-revelation to us as individuals. In every generation, the Wisdom of God enters into souls well-disposed to her:

> Though she is but one, she can do all things,
> and while remaining in herself, she renews all things;
> in every generation she passes into holy souls
> and makes them friends of God, and prophets;
> for God loves nothing so much as the man who lives
> with wisdom.
> For she is more beautiful than the sun,
> and excels every constellation of the stars.
> Compared with the light she is found to be superior,
> for it is succeeded by the night,
> but against wisdom evil does not prevail. (Wisdom 7: 27–30)

My hope is to reach any who are open right now to the light of this beauty, those currently searching, or those wanting to go deeper into what they've already heard to be true or know to be true.

If our Lord says "Behold, I make all things new!" (Rev 21:5) and yet the world and its things seem the same as ever, we should not write it off as wishful thinking or make-believe to have faith in his renewal. In fact, it is a golden opportunity for contemplation, for seeing what Jesus says only those who believe in him can see (See: Jn 12:46). The same Lord who opened the eyes of the blind still shines as the Light, not only of the ancient world of Palestine, but of our world today.

So that even if people are still people, and the world operates according to all the patterns Ecclesiastes says it does, with sunrise and sunset, rivers flowing to the sea, and the birth and death of all living things (See: Eccl 1, 3), we should look deeper for an inner renewal caused by grace. Change without grace, renovation without interior renewal, is spiritually worthless. The thing remodeled, so to speak, remains what it always was. The most important kind of regeneration isn't outward or skin-deep but takes place in the hidden depths of the soul.

At a certain point everyone revisits his or her faith with questions, fascination, or a deep hunger for meaning in life. That trip can be like visiting a museum or like a family reunion. It may start out cautiously, with hands clasped behind the back, taking care not to touch anything. You may stick to the outskirts of a gathering where it seems everyone knows everyone else, except you. You may prefer to observe rather than involve yourself. But if you are even slightly open to the Lord, you may find yourself not only welcomed but already understood by those inside the family circle. They were outsiders too, strangers and aliens at one time, before they were called in to enjoy communion.

So then you are no longer strangers and sojourners, but you are fellow citizens with the saints and members of the household of God, built upon the foundation of the apostles and prophets, Christ Jesus himself being the cornerstone, in whom the whole structure is joined together and grows into a holy temple in the Lord; in whom you also are built into it for a dwelling place of God in the Spirit. (Eph 2:19–22)

Apart from Jesus himself, the bridegroom for whom the ultimate eschatological banquet is thrown by his Father, you will find this festival peopled with saints who know you, and whom you—strangely, inexplicably—know better than you could have imagined. You will find a Mother who has not only been awaiting your arrival, but has been guiding it all along behind the scenes.

"There are two ways of getting home," writes Chesterton, "and one of them is to stay there. The other is to walk round the whole world till we come back to the same place."[5] Whether you've never left the household of the Faith or have beaten paths in all directions, the road we are all traveling on, however it bends, can bring us all home if we surrender to the guidance of him who says "I am the way" (Jn 14:6).

---

5 *Everlasting Man*, Preface.

CHAPTER ONE
The Story of Your Life

However scattered it looks, everything in the world fits in. Everyone with his own private history merges with the history of mankind, with the history of God's providence. Nothing … is in the strictest sense 'lost.' If it goes astray it can always be found again. It can be restored to where it belongs.

—HUBERT VAN ZELLER[1]

I f you go on retreat or to a penance service, any place where many confessions are heard, you're likely to hear this announcement: *When you go in for confession, just confess your sins. Don't tell Father your whole life story!* The point is not that your life story isn't worth telling, but that other people are standing in line behind you who also want their sins forgiven. But why is it even an issue? Why is it so easy to slip into *autobiography mode*?

The young often wonder: *How come old people tell so many stories?*

1   Hubert van Zeller, *The Will of God in Other Words* (Springfield, Ill.: Templegate Publishers, 1964), p. 87.

How come they tell the same stories over and over again? The answer isn't the same for both questions. But the older you get the more you realize: They tell stories because they've got stories to tell. And they want to tell them. Something about our human experience demands a retelling to another. Something about the recounting makes us feel unburdened of the past, relieved, heard, and understood.

Although looking back over our lives can sometimes feel like tumbling down a rabbit hole, what St. Josemaría Escrivá says of God's mercies makes all the crooked ways straight:

> The life of a man who lives by Faith will always be the story of the mercies of God. At some moments the story may perhaps be difficult to read, because everything can seem useless and even a failure. But at other times our Lord lets one see how the fruit abounds and then it is natural for one's soul to break out in thanksgiving.[2]

"The life of a man who lives by Faith will always be the story of the mercies of God." At the outset of these reflections on the mysteries of our faith and our place in them, such simplicity of approach is a must. With Scripture and the saints for our guides, we need to be on the lookout for a basic pattern woven throughout our lives. And just as the Bible rumbles with the one main theme of divine mercy, our lives also echo the divine thunderclap of clemency at times and places we never thought to listen for it. In God's own words: "In

2   Josemaría Escrivá, *Conversations with Josemaría Escrivá* (New York: Scepter, 2002), no. 72.

distress you called, and I rescued you; Unseen, I answered you in thunder" (Ps 81:8).[3] Like Saul toppled on the road to Damascus, those on the receiving end of mercy are often left shaken, but wide open to whatever God asks next.

Whenever the saints tell their stories, it is usually only upon request or under obedience. They don't typically enjoy speaking about themselves. But for them, ultimately, the story isn't really about themselves. It is all about glorifying the providence and mercy that has guided their steps. "But I received mercy" is how St. Paul punctuates the narrative of his former blaspheming, persecution, and insulting of Christ (1 Tm 1:12–14). *Blasphemy, persecution, insults*— those are his words, recorded for the sake of all who would come to believe in Christ with clouds hanging over them, with the baggage of guilt in tow.

To claim that our autobiographies are stories of mercy and love, however, does not mean that every event will look like an interlocking piece, nor that every happening will conform to our concept of merciful love. We have to be prepared to contemplate events that seem to bear no resemblance to it. Sometimes God's love is painful. Sometimes mercy feels like fire. Sometimes we cannot explain how or why we have ended up the way we are, much less justify it to ourselves. Those painful chapters of failure and uselessness St. Josemaría speaks of are among the most difficult to read.

Yet saints such as St. John Paul II, whose very lengthy and full

3   Confraternity translation.

life visibly concluded not only with the debilities of age but with the effects of Parkinson's, could say with unquestionable authority to the elderly, those in the evening of life, that love explains everything:

> Perhaps some of you remember times of pain and the hopes that never quite materialized. But all of us—to use the words of the First Letter of Saint John—"know and believe the love God has for us." Yes, God has loved and continues to love each one of you in a deep and personal way. *If you think back, you will see that your whole life is a story of God's love coming upon you in successive stages.* Life itself is a gift of the Father's love, as was your baptism, your Christian faith and the presence of the Holy Spirit down through the years. For all these gifts we sing a hymn of gratitude to God: "Blessed be the Lord who has shown me the wonders of his love."[4]

Better we should review our lives as the pope suggests: as an *overview* more than a series of random, isolated moments. All by themselves, the parts scarcely yield a unified picture. Considering them together, however, you find the story narrating itself as a ballad of mercy and praise. To read our lives, in other words, as we would salvation history is the task: as a whole, illumined by the light of Christ.

The Biblical story of Judah and Tamar is a case in point (See: Gen 38). The account of the patriarch Judah artlessly soliciting his

---

4   John Paul II, Address to the Elderly, Perth (Australia), (November 30, 1986), 2; italics added, http://w2.vatican.va/content/john-paul-ii/en/speeches/1986/november/documents/hf_jp-ii_spe_19861130_anziani-perth-australia.html.

daughter-in-law Tamar (albeit disguised as a prostitute) is startling for its nonchalance. Granted, not everything recorded in Scripture is for imitation, but we are left wondering why this episode of casual indulgence is recounted at all. It is not perhaps until the coming of Christ that the full import of this event comes to light: St. Matthew lists the illicit offspring of Judah and Tamar, the twins Perez and Zerah, as ancestors of Jesus Christ (Mt 1:3). They were links in a chain whose end could not be fully appreciated until the fullness of time had come.

As we revisit the Scriptures in these pages, a marvelous orchestration will appear that even the principal players themselves could not fully comprehend at the time. Yet the invariable response of God's holy ones will always remain our model: total surrender. Not comprehension, but surrender. The Marian question, "How can this be?" may well fall from our lips, so long as the supremely Marian response issues from our hearts: "Let it be to me according to your word" (Lk 1:38).

We are not only called to join the ranks of New Testament saints such as our Lady, St. Joseph, and St. Peter, but also those ancients whose first yeses prepared the way for their surrender: Abraham, Moses, Jonah, and so many others who had to walk by a deep faith that, nevertheless, didn't render them immune from uncertainty or even the occasional protest.

St. John Henry Newman characterizes ancient Israel's dependence on the Lord as a weighty command to follow in patience and trust:

It was a lesson continually set before the Israelites, that they were never to presume to act of themselves, but to wait till God wrought for them, to look on reverently, and then follow His guidance. God was their All-wise King: it was their duty to have no will of their own, distinct from His will, to form no plan of their own, to attempt no work of their own. "*Be still, and know that I am God.*" Move not, speak not—look to the pillar of the cloud, see how *it* moves—then follow. Such was the command.[5]

This teaches us a crucial truth: *Surrender in faith to merciful love is not only where the saint ends up; it is the very road on which he or she travels.* More than the end of the way, it is the way. And it is in the traveling, together with the Lord, that the relationship between him and the soul grows to maturity, the surrender becomes more wholehearted and secure. Whenever Jesus calls individuals in the Gospels, it is always to *follow* him, because it is only in the following that the proper relationship between Master and disciple can become what it was meant to be: a deep, intimate, trusting friendship whose hallmark is surrender.

More depends on surrender than it may seem. When we surrender to someone or something we admit its power over us, or we give it that power. And this can be a good or bad development: indicating freedom and maturity, on the one hand, or capitulation

5 John Henry Newman, "Wilfulness of Israel in Rejecting Samuel," in *Parochial and Plain Sermons*, vol. 3 (London: J. G. & F. Rivington, 1836), p. 17.

and hopelessness on the other. Hubert van Zeller frames it as a life choice in which our very identity hangs in the balance:

> All souls are made for God, but each goes by a unique way. Each has to decide whether to surrender to something less than God—and so becoming if not a slavish imitation a diminished person—or to surrender to the will of wisdom itself and finding identity and freedom.[6]

This is no less true if our sense of guilt effectively thwarts our approach to God. Surrender is not simply a high-level choice reserved to the spiritual elite. For many, it is the first step they need to take. St. Cyril of Jerusalem (315–386), in addressing the legitimate misgivings especially encountered by catechumens, really speaks to a barrier more or less every Christian comes up against.

> God is a lover of man, and a lover in no small measure. For do not say: "I have been a fornicator and an adulterer, I have committed grievous sin, and not once but very often; will He not forgive? Will He not grant pardon?" The sum of your sins does not surpass the magnitude of God's mercies. Your wounds are not beyond the healing skill of the great Physician. *Only surrender to Him with faith*, tell the Physician of your malady.[7]

---

6   Hubert van Zeller, *The Will of God in Other Words*, p. 74.

7   Cyril of Jerusalem: Lenten Lectures (*Catecheses*), Catechesis II, 6. *The Fathers of the Church: The Works of St. Cyril of Jerusalem*, vol. 1, trans. Leo McCauley and Anthony Stephenson (Washington, D.C.: The Catholic University of America Press, 1969), p. 99; italics added.

If up until now someone has wrestled against the Lordship of Christ and the demands of the Gospel, somewhat like Jacob against the angel, this book is a call for a truce. For whatever natural satisfaction comes from sparring, challenging, or resisting—nothing fulfills us more than self-surrender, the laying down of arms so as to embrace and be embraced.

Because even if our modern democratic world takes for granted the supreme value of radical individualism, Scripture and the saints continue to raise objections. Newman, again, presses the issue. Even if the young revel in the feeling of self-determination, Newman asks, "Is it any happiness, or any comfort, to consider that we *are* our own?"[8] If we are honest, even the most individualistic will admit a feeling of imbalance and even of selfishness in living on their own terms. "As time goes on," Newman continues, the young and independent, "as all men, will find that independence was not made for man—that it is an unnatural state—may do for a while, but will not carry us on safely to the end."[9]

What will carry us "safely" home, then, is not forcing the rudder ourselves, much less trying to change the direction of the wind. It is surrender to him who, so to speak, steers our boat in ways that require faith and trust. Jesus accompanies us inconspicuously as a fellow passenger. Though a carpenter by trade, he offers advice as to how we should fish. He sometimes even falls asleep on a cushion in

8 John Henry Newman, "Remembrance of Past Mercies," in *Parochial and Plain Sermons*, vol. 5 (London: Longmans, Green, and Co., 1899), p. 83.

9 Newman, p. 84.

the stern. Occasionally, he does not bother using a boat at all even in crossing even turbulent waters, but goes on foot. There may also come a day when he bids us to join him on those waters! But the boat always arrives at the shore to which it is heading because of him whom even the wind and sea obey.

If nothing else, this divine arrangement demands much prayer from us, that contemplation of which we spoke earlier. The apostles often initially responded to Jesus' mode of leadership (or *Lordship*) aboard the boat with cries for help, deliverance, even with complaints. But each moment of surprise or panic was crafted by Christ to teach faithful dependence, a lesson each of them eventually learned. We cannot forget that this is still how the Lord makes disciples, learners of us, by moving us from self-reliance and independence to a state more "natural" to us: childlike confidence and dependence.

If the consistent (and heroic) disposition of saints of all times and places is this surrender, then it is perhaps unfortunate that the idea primarily evokes images of battle and war. One side clearly has the upper hand and the other must give up or risk complete destruction. But there is another surrender; that of love, as in marriage or friendship. It is not one will forcing itself upon another or dominating the other. It isn't a fight: "I give up. You win." It is a mutual desire to give the gift of self.

Pope Benedict XVI, in commemorating his own anniversary of priestly ordination, spoke of the priesthood in terms of friendship with Christ, in the language of surrender:

He knows me by name. I am not just some nameless being in the infinity of the universe. He knows me personally. Do I know him? The friendship that he bestows upon me can only mean that I too try to know him better; that in the Scriptures, in the Sacraments, in prayer, in the communion of saints, in the people who come to me, sent by him, I try to come to know the Lord himself more and more.

Friendship is not just about knowing someone; it is above all a communion of the will. It means that my will grows into ever greater conformity to his will. For his will is not something external and foreign to me, something to which I more or less willingly submit or else refuse to submit. No, in friendship, my will grows together with his will, and his will becomes mine: this is how I become truly myself.[10]

That is the type of surrender that God asks of us, and that the events and circumstances of our lives are the ever-present occasion. He found this high level of submission in Mary's perpetual willingness to listen carefully and say yes without worry or reservation. I don't think we can fully appreciate our Lady's faith and generosity, nor that of any of the other saints of biblical and Church history, until we commit ourselves to the same exacting work of self-surrender. As Pope Benedict also says, "At a deep level, the essence of love, the

---

10 Homily of His Holiness Benedict XVI, Vatican Basilica (June 29, 2011), http://w2.vatican.va/content/benedict-xvi/en/homilies/2011/documents/hf_ben-xvi_hom_20110629_pallio.html.

essence of genuine fruit, coincides with the idea of setting out, going towards: it means self-abandonment, self-giving, it bears within itself the sign of the cross."[11]

This prepares us to read our own life stories, our itineraries from home to where we are now: all of the stops we've made along the way, the choices, the accomplishments, the failures, as a journey under the watchful eye of the God who is Love. That Love draws from us the crucial surrender that renders us not only more pleasing to him, but more truly ourselves. "What is love," asks Newman, "but a delight in God, a devotion to Him, a surrender of the whole self to Him?"[12]

If Pope Benedict insists that love at its deepest level means "setting out, going towards" in self-giving and self-abandonment, then our life journey to God might very well parallel God's journey to us in Christ, sent as man by the Father to give his life as a ransom for us. And indeed the Gospels teem with examples of Jesus going out of his way for the sake of the lost, although nothing about his mission among us is truly off-course for him. The mission of the God-Man is, by his definition, a seeking after the wayward and abandoned.

That the Good Shepherd leaves "the ninety-nine sheep in the wilderness, and [goes] after the one which is lost, until he finds it," or that the good Samaritan turns aside to dress the wounds of the battered and abandoned traveler, or even that Jesus inserts himself

11 Ibid.

12 John Henry Newman, "Purity and Love," in *Discourses Addressed to Mixed Congregations* (London: Longmans, Green, and Co., 1899), p. 62.

among "tax collectors and sinners" at table, reveals that "[Jesus] has come to us with a heart made of flesh, a heart like ours."[13] He has come in search of us that we might journey in search of him, with the confidence of people who are loved.

This is why the human heart of our Savior is the key that unlocks many of the mysteries of our lives: our joys, our heartbreaks, our sorrows, our everything. And we have to see our place in that Heart. It may be helpful to see it not so much as our destination but as our cradle or refuge, as the support that carries us safely to our end. We must know that we have a place there, have always had a place, and will always have a place.

It is worth reminding ourselves, especially if our lives feel particularly fragmented, that Providence passes through the human heart of the Savior. Providence is not only about seeing how a huge, complicated plan works. It's not about seeing how all the pieces of my life go together, how I am a part of something incomprehensibly complex and great. Yes, this is a marvelous thing. But, more importantly, providence is how God personally loves me, how he saves me. It is how he uses me to build up his kingdom and save others. Even when my eyes are blind to the purpose of God's will, faith assures me that divine designs and intentions are still operative—perhaps not to be understood, but surrendered to.

Newman uncompromisingly assures us:

> We are not sent into this world for nothing; we are not born

13 Josemaría Escrivá, *Christ is Passing By* (New York: Scepter, 2002), no. 162.

at random; we are not here, that we may go to bed at night, and get up in the morning, toil for our bread, eat and drink, laugh and joke, sin when we have a mind, and reform when we are tired of sinning, rear a family and die. God sees every one of us; He creates every soul, He lodges it in the body, one by one, for a purpose. He needs, He deigns to need, every one of us. He has an end for each of us; we are all equal in His sight, and we are placed in our different ranks and stations, not to get what we can out of them for ourselves, but to labour in them for Him. As Christ has His work, we too have ours; as He rejoiced to do His work, we must rejoice in ours also.[14]

Such assurance is incomprehensible without faith. To see life without faith, taking everything at face value only, the alternatives are both stark and disappointing: good luck and bad, winners and losers. Some people get all the breaks; others pay all the bills. Some always feel like they're trying to catch up with everyone else; others feel like they've missed something somewhere along the line. Some feel like they're forever suffering the consequences of the sins and mistakes of their youth; others, that they're continually suffering from the consequences of other people's sins. In the end, you have a story without resolution, even without a plot.

But when someone undergoes a deep conversion, a surprisingly coherent narrative often reveals itself. Everything that had seemed

14 John Henry Newman, "God's Will the End of Life," in *Discourses Addressed to Mixed Congregations*, pp.111–2.

meaningless, arbitrary, or random suddenly appears textured, ordered, even willed. Past events were a prelude, a backstory, to a life-changing encounter with the living God. *A mind and a heart have been quietly but consistently directing my life.* Discerning what God has been doing all along inspires awe and fascination: *What has my pre-conversion life amounted to? How did I end up on my knees in prayer?*

The consistent testimony of saints and saintly people is to attribute everything to the divine mercy. And since modern people tend to pay greater attention to personal witness over words alone, as St. Paul VI once said, we look to saints who actually lingered in sin before finding the path home—those who tasted the sweetness of the Lord only after having drunk to the dregs of vice.

Although we will cite several examples of saints who have told their stories to the world, for now let us listen to the voice of one on the heels of whose amazing conversion came an equally radical call to follow Christ. Blessed Charles de Foucauld (1858–1916) lost both of his parents by the age of six, and then lost his faith in later youth. A number of years of dissolute living followed, eventually resulting in his dismissal from the army for conduct unbecoming. After conversion, he pursued a monastic and uniquely eremitical vocation, ending up a missionary priest in the Sahara, where he lived and died in the greatest humility and poverty, respected by Christians and non-Christians alike. The Tuareg people in whose midst he served were represented at St. Peter's Basilica when Benedict XVI beatified him in 2005.

Foucauld's autobiographical writings reveal a man totally overwhelmed by the mercies of God, as though he had been pursued by them from eternity:

> How many are your mercies, O God—mercies yesterday and today, and at every moment of my life, from before my birth, from before time itself began! I am plunged deep in mercies—I drown in them: they cover me, wrapping me round on every side.
>
> O God, we should all hymn the praises of your mercies—we, who were all created for everlasting glory and redeemed by the blood of Jesus....[15]

Yet it is only by contrasting this exalted hymn of praise with the depths of ennui and dissipation from which he had been rescued that we fully grasp the mercy of which he sings.

> You made me experience a melancholic emptiness, a sadness that I never felt at other times. It would come back to me every evening when I was alone in my rooms; it kept me silent and depressed during our so-called celebrations: I would organize them, but when time came, I went through them in silence, disgust and infinite boredom. You gave me the ill-defined unrest that marks an unquiet conscience which, though it may be wholly asleep, is not completely dead. I never felt that sadness, that distress, that restlessness apart from those times.

---

15 Charles de Foucauld, *The Spiritual Autobiography of Charles de Foucauld* (Ijamsville, Maryland: The Word Among Us Press, 2003), p. 10.

It was undoubtedly a gift from you, O God.[16]

His very contemporary-sounding words reveal a height of insight attained only in retrospect, in the light of grace. God had been involved all along, teasing a hunger and thirst for higher things from out of his emptiness.

Perhaps it all sounds very unlikely: God's gift in the form of a troubled conscience, dissatisfaction, and boredom. But it shows us how the saints reread their lives in the light of faith: mercy, grace, gift of God; it is all one. "We know that in everything," says St. Paul, "God works for good with those who love him, who are called according to his purpose" (Rom 8:28). Knowing this in theory is one thing, but experiencing it in one's life prompts praise like nothing else.

It is ordinarily harder to judge our own experience as a string of mercies than that of others. It is difficult seeing outside of our own experience. From the inside, all we see are knots and contradictions. When a friend consoles another in sorrow, it is often the outsider who sees the grace and mercy at work in the trial. Sometimes it takes another to tell us our own story, or at least to interpret it. If God is both outside and inside human experience, experiencing in Christ what is human more humanly than anyone, then we should listen carefully to what he says about it. And those who drink closest to the source of mercy, the saints, are the surest interpreters in helping us translate Providence into mercy.

From the vantage point of another holy man of the twentieth

16 de Foucauld, pp. 11–12.

century, Blessed Columba Marmion (1858–1923), we are refreshed to learn that "the mysteries of Christ are our mysteries." This saintly contemporary of de Foucauld assures us that all of the joyful, sorrowful, and glorious mysteries of Jesus' life were lived and experienced for us:

> ...what makes Christ's mysteries ours is, above all, because the Eternal Father saw us with His Son in each of the mysteries lived by Christ and because Christ accomplished them as Chief of the Church. I might even say that, on account of this, the mysteries of Christ Jesus are more our mysteries than they are His. Christ, inasmuch as He is the Son of God, would not have undergone the abasements of the Incarnation, the sorrows and sufferings of the Passion; He would have had no need of the triumph of the Resurrection, which succeeded the ignominy of His death. He went through all this as Head of the Church; He took upon Himself *our* miseries and *our* infirmities... He willed to pass through what we ourselves must pass through, and He merited for us the grace to follow after Him in each of His mysteries.[17]

Knowing that Jesus went through everything for us, although he had no need to, not only infuses all of our life events with meaning, but reveals how ready-to-hand is the grace to meet those events— especially the sorrowful ones. In fact, trauma recovery programs

17 Columba Marmion, OSB, *Christ in His Mysteries* (St. Louis, MO: B. Herder Book Co., 1919), pp. 14–15.

exist that seek to connect the participants' experience of physical and emotional trauma to those suffered by Christ on our behalf: the abuse of his body, his blindfolding and taunting, the disregard of his voice as he pleaded with merciless adversaries, his internal anguish over his passion and death, etc. By contemplation and desire, we need to find our place in all of these distressing mysteries, in each of his wounds, by which we are healed.

The One who sustains such injuries without protest so that I can arrive at peace and wholeness must have all the answers I'm looking for in life. The One who rises from death and passes through a locked door into an upper room filled with fearful men, to show himself to *me*, wounds and all, must have the answers I'm looking for, and must be himself the key. If this is the image that has come to embody the Divine Mercy, then it surely must speak to my uneven, patchwork, messy life, as the One through whom God reconciles all things (See: Col 1:20). My story must flow from him, and return to him.

CHAPTER TWO
The Deepest Truth about Ourselves: Baptism & Christian Identity

Do not forget: anyone who does not realize that he is a child of God is unaware of the deepest truth about himself.

–ST. JOSEMARÍA ESCRIVÁ[1]

I f you are willing to retrace the steps of your life under the light of God's love and mercy, willing to surrender to his providential care even if the details remain blurry, then you need to know an open secret about Christianity: Christian identity begins and ends with childhood—the unique childhood of the children of God. The pilgrim or wayfarer whose life is explained by mercy must be a child—not a worn-out, jaded, skeptical adult,

---

1 Josemaría Escrivá, *Friends of God* (New York: Scepter, 2002), no. 26.

but a child. Spiritually-speaking, our faith leaves us no choice: It's either the cradle or the grave. As Jesus warns us, "unless you turn and become like children, you will never enter the kingdom of heaven" (Mt 18:3). Never means never.

Our Lord undeniably wants our interior life revolutionized by this teaching, as he proved on one occasion in settling the apostles' dispute over which of them was the greatest (See: Lk 9:46–48; Mt 18:1–4). Jesus responded with a surprising but concrete visual aid. He inserted a child into the midst of grown men and, once all eyes and ears were trained on the spectacle, laid down the entrance requirement for his kingdom: *You will not enter the kingdom of God unless you become like this child.* To big, strong men who had other ideas about what it meant to be great, this was the answer they got. And Jesus leaves them and us to contemplate and apply the meaning: Somehow the child that we see *out there* in the arms of Jesus has to become who we are *on the inside*.

My friend, if you want to be great, become little.

To be little it is necessary to believe as children believe, to love as children love, to give yourself up as children give themselves up...to pray as children pray.[2]

If St. Josemaría's words challenge (or perplex) us as those of Jesus did the apostles, it is time to pray with the simplicity urged by the Lord and his holy ones. It is also time to get used to the saints shaking us out of our comfort zones. Almost always, the thing you least expect

2   Josemaría Escrivá, *Holy Rosary* (New York: Scepter, 2002), Author's Note.

will be the thing expected of you: strength through weakness, life through death, forgiveness instead of retaliation. The list of gospel surprises goes on, going totally against our worldly survival skills. But Jesus does not want a mass of mere survivors falling in behind him; he wants those who will learn to live *abundantly* by allowing the gospel to do its graceful work in their souls, through teachings that will often rub us the wrong way.

This is why we need to let spiritual childhood sink in as the necessity it is. Only the spiritual child can accept help from God, perceive the need for help, and not be ashamed of it. Only the child knows that he or she does not have all the answers. Only children rejoice in the mere fact of being alive. Only children can really pray. To become again as a little child may not automatically inspire security in us, but it is the one and only way we can follow the Lord with any kind of sincerity as we embrace "the risky security of the Christian."[3]

As Jesus jars us with the demands of his gospel, the saints follow suit by startling us with their insights into the basic truths of our faith. Until a holy person comes along and embodies the gospel, its radical demands might suffer the fate of a museum piece: safe under glass, to be admired but not handled. In saints we witness how grace works "in the flesh," transforming people like ourselves into icons of the living God, making the "ever ancient, ever new" quality of gospel teaching strike a new generation with its relevance and urgency.

Few saints have accomplished this with greater swiftness and

3   Escrivá, *Christ is Passing By*, no. 58.

scope than St. Thérèse of Lisieux (1873–1897). Venerable Pope Pius XII claimed that the young Carmelite had done no less than rediscover the Gospel for the modern world: "It is the Gospel itself, it is the heart of the Gospel that she rediscovered; but with what grace and freshness: 'If you do not become like children, you shall not enter the Kingdom of Heaven'" (Mt 18:3).[4]

To say that she had recovered not only a neglected truth but the very "heart of the Gospel" is like announcing that someone has unearthed the treasure buried in the field or found the pearl of great price. It suggests that the mysteries once spoken openly to the world by Christ have been received anew by one with ears to hear. And thus the ancient thunder of gospel teaching reechoes through the voice of an unlikely herald: a teenage girl cloistered from the world in a small Carmel located, not even in Paris, but in a forgotten French town.

St. Thérèse reintroduced modern people to what it means to be a child of God more than in name only. Her teaching may not come across in the sweeping, apocalyptic tenor of a prophet, nor with the urgency of a private revelation. Yet for those with ears to hear, the muted tones of her "little way" of spiritual childhood resonate with the equally subdued character of daily life. Woven of aspirations, trials, successes and setbacks, our daily experiences spontaneously converge in a cry for God's help. How often do we find ourselves

4   Radio Message of Pope Pius XII for the Consecration of the Basilica of Saint Thérèse of Lisieux: http://w2.vatican.va/content/pius-xii/fr/speeches/1954/documents/hf_p-xii_spe_19540711_lisieux.html.

needing and asking for strength—even courage—to make it through the ordinary duties and pressures of life?

St. Thérèse's little way defuses the distress that our weaknesses might cause by encouraging an open avowal of one's limitations. She declares: "It is so good to feel that one is weak and little!"[5] This is because Jesus reserves his saving mission for the lost, the sick, and the forsaken. When we recognize our place in one or all of those categories, then we reach the same conclusion as St. Paul who not only refused to conceal but *preferred* to boast of his weaknesses (See: 2 Cor 11:30; 12:9–10). St. Thérèse, in fact, explains her little way in accents similar to St. Paul: "It is to recognize our nothingness, to expect everything from God as a little child expects everything from its father … to be disquieted about nothing…."[6]

Although it is God's gift through baptismal adoption, spiritual childhood clearly demands serious effort. Naturally we become disquieted about many things; normally we're more prepared to hide our weaknesses than boast of them. But if being a child of God is rooted in God's fatherhood over us, in his strength, then the equation must conclude as Thérèse and so many other saints unanimously indicate. St. Josemaría, one of Thérèse's earliest devotees, calculates the enormous imbalance of power:

> Lord, you are who you are. I am nothingness itself. You have

5   Thérèse of Lisieux, *Her Last Conversations*, trans. J. Clarke, OCD (Washington, D.C.: Institute of Carmelite Studies, 1977), p. 74.

6   Escrivá, *Conversations*, p. 139.

all the perfections: power, strength, love, glory, wisdom, authority, dignity... If I unite myself to you, like a child who goes to the strong arms of his father or the wonderful lap of his mother, I will feel the warmth of your divinity, I will feel the light of your wisdom, I will feel your strength coursing through my veins.[7]

To be a child of God does not mean setting aside reason, life experience, street smarts, or anything else we've acquired in the course adult life. It means cultivating a spirit of trust and confidence in God in the face of life's hard-earned lessons. The spiritual child resists the pessimism and bitterness that often attach to age like barnacles. In making us adopted children of God, baptism does not make us passive or gullible, nor are we disconnected from the harsh realities of life. We are rather invited to embrace the strength, warmth, and wisdom of God as our defining qualities, not to present a hollow profile of worldly success and shrewdness as a counterfeit to character, but to know that our identity in Christ runs deeper than even the dearest qualities about ourselves: ethnicity, citizenship, group affiliations, etc. This is why St. Josemaría insists that our childhood in God is the "deepest truth" about ourselves. It's not all about appearances, but substance. Our personhood is at stake in what we hold to be the bedrock truth about ourselves.

But even for Christians this is strangely easy to overlook. Deep truths need to be lived deeply, and living beneath the surface demands

7   Josemaría Escrivá, *The Forge* (New York: Scepter, 2002), no. 342.

an effort best called contemplative. We can't fully appreciate the implications of baptism, much less see the Lord's fingerprints all over our lives, unless we're willing to look closely and prayerfully at ourselves and the world around us with "discerning eye," to borrow a phrase from Emily Dickinson.

Scripture contrasts human appearances with the hidden contents of the heart to show that God alone really knows the heart, even better than the one in whose chest it beats. God searches and judges us in that place, where our thoughts and desires and motivations lay bare before him. But because it is such a "tortuous" and incomprehensible place for us to be (See: Jer 17:9–10), we find it less troublesome to live on the outside.

It is easier, consequently, to pin our identity on things external—from our looks, to the esteem of others, to whatever successes we may credit to ourselves—and call it *me*. For some this even takes a downward turn, taking a personal defect or sin and telling themselves: "This is me. This is all I'm good for." More than merely a personal problem, taking the part for the whole is the epidemic of a culture where image is everything. Many features of our personalities are good; some are undoubtedly not. Not one taken all by itself *is* the self. Taking one good quality or one defect and setting it up as "who I am" distorts the human person into a caricature.

If you're going to choose one characteristic and call it you, it should be the deepest characteristic—the truth that God planted first in you and formed everything else around. Our adoption as his children is that truth, that reality, which can never be lost, replaced, or substituted. It is our reference point in all things. Some may consider this a kind of benign, "nonthreatening" truth, more consoling than demanding. If it helps you to think of baptism this way, that's okay for now. We first need to receive the gift as a gift before discerning the most fitting way to use it, according to the mind of the giver. In fact, many remain shallow in their Christian faith from simple neglect to receive this truth into their hearts. It may sound too basic and simple to merit prayerful consideration more than once, if at all.

But failure to live deeply in this reality, neglecting to contemplate it, exposes us to the temptation of opting for merely cosmetic solutions to settle the issue of our self-worth. And since "our outer nature is wasting away," we need to make sure that "our inner nature is being renewed every day" by something substantial (See: 2 Cor 4:16). It's no good to make ourselves dependent on another's affirmations, inspirational sayings, motivational music, etc., to put us in a place of confidence and peace. By all means, receive affirmation graciously, make use of inspirational sayings, images, and songs. But avoid so stringing them together that they form a diversion from your inner poverty. There is an undeniable emptiness within us all, a void fillable by God alone. He knows it's there: the Lord created it for himself as his "personal space." Ignorant of its purpose, we dread its presence, and try to forget or fill it the best we can. But until we acknowledge it, and try to figure out what God wants us to do with it, we doom ourselves to a more or less continual fruitless search for substitutes, novelty, a distraction.

This is a point to which spiritual writers frequently return, and there's no need to break ranks with them here. So many of our problems, so much lack of peace, stem from trying to fill old wineskins or patch a worn-out garment with new material. What is needed is a new vessel altogether, and this God has given us with a new heart and a new spirit in baptism. But we need to treat it as such. St. Paul frequently feels the need to remind the first generation of Christians about this:

> Do you not know that the unrighteous will not inherit the kingdom of God? ... And such were some of you. But you were washed, you were sanctified, you were justified in the name of the Lord Jesus Christ and in the Spirit of our God.
>
> The body is not meant for immorality, but for the Lord, and the Lord for the body....Do you not know that your bodies are members of Christ? Shall I therefore take the members of Christ and make them members of a prostitute? Never! Do you not know that he who joins himself to a prostitute becomes one body with her?...But he who is united to the Lord becomes one spirit with him. Shun immorality. Every other sin which a man commits is outside the body; but the immoral man sins against his own body. (See: 1 Cor 6:9–20)

Our desire for God will never deepen, much less find fulfillment, if our house, our inner dwelling place, is always being remodeled, repurposed from a sanctuary to something profane, or even tottering and collapsing. If the Lord tells the apostles to avoid restless wandering, "moving from house to house" in their journeys, this also reveals how much God values stability in us. He wants to put down roots in rooted people, so that the roots, intertwining, can grow together. He wants us to give him "room to grow," which really means the widening of our capacity for him.

Contemporary trends in identity-seeking are unquestionably disconcerting, discussions of changeable gender identity being among the most disturbing. Hubert van Zeller has already observed in the early 1980s: "People change their jobs, their houses, their cars, their wives and husbands, if possible their physical appearances in a way probably not equaled in any other period of history."[8] Changes of these kinds bespeak a widespread restlessness, a lack of contentment with self, and want of purpose and direction in life. We've even stopped asking why people do these things. Many stop at the surface and figure it's just a matter of preferences and choices. If you can choose one thing or another, choice is its own justification.

But our basic insecurity about selfhood points to our positive need for that bedrock foundation upon which Jesus says our house must be built if we would not be swept away when the storms of life rage against us. We could consider the sand he warns us against as the insubstantial, wobbly footing of personal qualities that run no deeper than, say, a tattoo. The impression of permanence, of character, of being "all in" may be given, but there's no real power presiding over how we think about ourselves on the deepest level.

8   Hubert van Zeller, *Spirituality Recharted* (Petersham, Mass.: St. Bede's Publications, 1985), p. 153.

The Son of God became the Son of Man to teach us all about who we are in God's eyes, and where our renewed identity should lead us. Vatican Council II beautifully described the mission of Jesus in these terms:

Only in the mystery of the incarnate Word does the mystery of man take on light. Christ, the final Adam, by the revelation of the mystery of the Father and His love, fully reveals man to man himself and makes his supreme calling clear. (*Gaudium et Spes*, no. 22)

Our *supreme calling* begins by recognizing Jesus as our ideal, our role model in all things. The imitation of Christ is the most fundamental call of the Gospel. After we have heeded the call to repentance, which must always precede and accompany friendship with the Lord, we are not left in the dark as to our next move: "If anyone serves me, he must follow me; and where I am, there shall my servant be also" (Jn 12:26). And in the process of following and abiding with Jesus, we imbibe his spirit: "Take my yoke upon you, and learn from me; for I am gentle and lowly in heart, and you will find rest for your souls" (Mt 11:29).

The soulful rest we seek—in looking for ourselves, in seeking someone capable of explaining what our lives mean, in searching for a savior to save us from our incompleteness and frailty—is resolved in Jesus. This discovery is nowhere more poignantly sketched than in the Lord's interactions with the wounded and world-weary of the Gospels. The Samaritan woman of John 4 occupies a striking place among them, as her sometimes uneasy dialogue with the Lord concludes with nothing short of a personal revolution. We will return to her in another chapter, but to draw out one point for now: if this woman's transformation in the space of a single conversation is recorded for our instruction, it is also recounted for our imitation.

The Gospels abound with individuals whose needs and problems are unique to them, and yet always universal enough to meet us at whatever stage we are in our journey. But the "role models" whom the Gospels propose for our imitation are not always what you would expect. Their true worth cannot be appreciated except with a contemplative, discerning eye.

Among others, the aspiring disciple is thrown in among the good Samaritan, a dishonest steward, a penitent woman who makes an embarrassing display of herself at a dinner party with perfumed ointment, a persistent widow, another woman who won't take no for an answer when the apostles beg the Lord to send her away....

Is there a common denominator behind all these unlikely role models? How can a clever but dishonest steward join forces with the selfless Samaritan? How can the widow who claims her rights before a reluctant judge find common ground with the penitent woman who appeals for nothing but mercy from the Savior?

In some way, everything is resolved in the child of God. More than any others, little children are the Lord's favored scale-model of the Christian. Unless we become like the ones who crawled up to and clung to Jesus and received his blessing, we won't get anywhere spiritually, nor will we understand the boldness of those who throw themselves at the Lord in ways that seem shameless. The character profile, the identity, of the child of God is that of the penitent, the lover, the persistent—all have a pleasing confidence that wins the heart of the Savior.

What parents have always told their children, "Tell me who your friends are and I'll tell you who you are," is a good reminder for us to imitate these gospel patterns of childhood and discipleship. Everyone searches for self. Children instinctively look up to their elders and peers, to those who strike them as good, heroic, expert, or even just *cool*. But the axiom of spiritual writers that "we become what we love," tells us that we must choose our friends, our role models, wisely.

Loving, after all, means willing, wanting; and our character is formed more by our choices than anything else. A great Doctor of the Church such as St. Augustine could say that he loved God not as something vague, or "with some vague feeling," but with assurance and confidence (See: *Confessions* 10, 6). And this was the same saint whose dramatic conversion was all about identity. His reading of St. Paul's "put on the Lord Jesus Christ" settled everything for him (Rom 13:14).

There exists no deeper truth about us than that: having put on the Lord Jesus Christ, our identity is renewed in God's beloved Son. The adults against whom Jesus contrasts God's children are those sunk in the pitfalls of age: skepticism, over-thinking, second-guessing, and self-reliance. We find these types berating Jesus for associating with sinners or dumfounded over his preference for the smallest and least among men. But the Gospel is unambiguous: In the same breath, Jesus couples "that you may be sons of your Father who is in heaven" with "be perfect, as your heavenly Father is perfect" (See: Mt 5:43–48).

St. John, the Lord's beloved friend and disciple, takes great pains to explain how the coming of Christ in the flesh should change our entire outlook: the way we see God and self, our spirituality, our way of thinking. Since he was closest to Christ, and *so knew* himself to be loved by the Lord as to refer to himself as the one "whom Jesus loved," we can almost feel him taking us by the arm as he introduces us to our new identity in Christ: "See what love the Father has given us, that we should be called children of God; and so we are…. Beloved, we are God's children now" (1 Jn 3:1–2). These words still sound fresh, urgent, and attractive to us after two thousand years, and they should.

But for many Christians it's as though they're missing something very basic, something that should be obvious, something that ought to mark clearly how they think, act, and speak; a reality that should bring them assurance of love, peace, and unbounded confidence in God. Sometimes even good and faithful believers will admit that, although they believe in God's love for them and in their status as his adopted children, it remains largely a theory. They do not "feel" it and so do not think, act, and pray as beloved children.

We have observed that, in general, people struggle with their identity. Mostly as a result of original sin, people frequently want to be something other than what they are. Adam and Eve were God's beloved children, but reached after a "higher" status independent of God, making themselves his competitors, as it were. The contemporary spiritual writer Fr. Jacques Philippe mentions how people often want to be *more of* something: more attractive, more intelligent, more respected, more virtuous, more free, more talented, etc.[9] This can point to a fundamental insecurity about ourselves or a broader dissatisfaction about how our lives are turning out.

If we are not careful, these desires (which *can* be good) might amount to our not wanting to have to rely on anyone or anything, not even on God himself. We want to be self-sufficient and self-made, to impress the world by our own resourcefulness and innate personal strength. But this is all a part of the original lie that beguiled our first parents and that too often has the power to tempt us. God does not call us to be his children because we are beautiful, persuasive, eloquent, charming, intelligent, or especially talented. We might be all of those things and more, but that is not why God calls us to be his children, nor is it why God loves us.

God makes us his children so that he can love us as our Father, so that he can share his goodness in the most abundant way possible. Children are in the best position possible to receive: everything that they need must come from their parents. Just so, the Lord wants us to rest spiritually in that same dependent position, so that he can give as a Father gives and we can receive as children receive.

In the poignant Christmas sermon cited in the previous

9   Jacques Philippe, *The Way of Trust and Love* (New York: Scepter, 2012), pp. 44–45.

chapter[10], St. John Henry Newman reflects on "this season, when we are engaged in celebrating God's grace in making us His children, by the incarnation of His Only-begotten Son, the greatest and most wonderful of all His mercies." It is in that context, as Newman probes into man's unholy drive for independence, that he unmasks independence as a spiritually unsafe and humanly unnatural state for us. To deny what God wills us to be sets us up not only for frustration but even for disaster.

Christian spirituality takes divine *filiation* or *sonship* as its primary point of departure, making us consciously dependent on God for absolutely everything. St. Josemaría regards this simply as a matter of justice: "If you are really striving to be just, you will often reflect on your utter dependence upon God, and be filled with gratitude and the desire to repay the favors of a Father who loves us to the point of madness."[11]

This is what it means to be a child of God: depending, trusting, taking risks for God; this is what our baptism leads us to as his children. No one can compel us to *feel* one way or another about our divine filiation, because our status as adopted children does not depend upon something as mutable as our moods and feelings. But to act in faith according to this deepest truth about ourselves brings us an experiential conviction that God is "our Father, and very

10 "Remembrance of Past Mercies."

11 Escriva, *Friends of God*, 167.

much our Father, ... who is both near us and in heaven."[12]

We find that God is faithful when we do as the beloved Son of God did in his life upon earth. Directly after his baptism, Jesus put himself in a position of utter dependence on his heavenly Father, when he "was led by the Spirit for forty days in the wilderness, tempted by the devil. And he ate nothing in those days; and when they were ended, he was hungry" (Lk 4:1–2). Our Lord was strong, fearless, and trusting, even while suffering the debilities consequent upon fasting. He did this to teach us what it looks and feels like to be the children of God. It is always the same: littleness and weakness buttressed by a power that subtly sustains, without removing our feeling of inadequacy. In a sense, we need to feel fragile even as we overcome obstacles.

The divine pleasure that the heavenly Father voiced upon Jesus' baptism, however, is the affirmation that underwrites all of our childlike confidence. As Jesus journeyed into the unforgiving desert terrain to be tempted by the devil, he still had ringing in his ears the Father's voice: "This is my beloved Son, with whom I am well pleased" (Mt 3:17).

Humanly speaking, when someone knows that he is loved or admired by another, there is a feeling of humble confidence, of joy, of strength and courage. *I am seen by another who takes pleasure in me.* And the last thing we want is to be rebellious and independent. Union, love, and self-giving are all we can think of.

12 See: Josemaría Escrivá, *The Way, The Forge, Furrow* (New York: Scepter, 2011), no. 267.

On the supernatural level, we take this a step further. The evident failure of all creatures to love us completely compels us to depend on God alone for our security. We have to be entirely swept away by the truth that God looks upon us with perfect love, always love, and only love: "In this is love, not that we loved God but that he loved us" (1 Jn 4:10). Everything else in our lives should flow from that golden truth: our prayer, our work, our interpersonal relationships.

Our baptism initiates us into this mystery of God's love for us, because in it the Father's love is *impressed* within us, a love that he never removes. What St. Josemaría calls the "deepest truth" about ourselves means exactly this: In the Lord's baptism our own status as God's children is shown forth. As the Holy Spirit descends upon Jesus and the Father declares his pleasure in his Son, the deepest truth about our identity is revealed: we too are God's beloved children, whose calling it is to receive gratefully the love that he pours into us, desiring *to repay the favors of a Father who loves us to the point of madness.*

CHAPTER THREE
The Way In: The Holy Spirit

How lovely is thy dwelling place, O LORD of hosts!

–PSALM 84:1

Whenever I give retreats to cloistered nuns, I always tell them something they already know from experience: Although it's difficult to restrict your life to cloister boundaries, it's even harder to be a contemplative. Identifying oneself as either "cloistered" or "secular," removed from the world or immersed in it, is as easy as declaring one's eye color. Calling yourself a contemplative is more elusive. It's all on the inside.

All religious, cloistered or not, have observances that serve to protect their inner life: silence and solitude, fasting and vigils, and *lectio divina* (or sacred reading) are among the most important. But safeguard and foster is all that they're supposed to do, or can do, for the interior life. They promote it, but cannot make it happen. Everyone who prays knows what it's like to be in peaceful silence, even in a remote and ideal venue, and yet to find themselves interiorly disquieted, emotionally all over the map. Circumstances may help or hinder, but they do not decide the quality of our prayer.

If devout lay people struggle to be contemplatives in the midst of the world, it might dishearten them to learn that even those chosen out of this world must do battle on the same front. For those who live in the mix of the world, as for those whose lives observe the quiet rhythms of the monastery, the essential itinerary is the same: the journey inward, seeking God in the soul. Before you can begin to find God *out there*, in the people and events of daily life, you must first recognize him *within*.

St. John of the Cross considers this insight decisive: Once you realize your own beauty and dignity as God's privileged dwelling place, you will spare no effort to meet him there, hidden within.

> Oh, then, soul, most beautiful among all creatures, so anxious to know the dwelling place of your Beloved so you may go in search of him and be united with him, now we are telling you that you yourself are his dwelling and his secret inner room and hiding place. …

> Since you know now that your desired Beloved lives hidden within your heart, strive to be really hidden with him, and you will embrace him within you and experience him with loving affection.[1]

---

1 John of the Cross, *The Spiritual Canticle*, stanza 1.7, 10, in *The Collected Works of St. John of the Cross*, trans. Kieran Kavanaugh and Otilio Rodriguez, rev. ed. (Washington, D.C.: ICS, 1991), pp. 480–1.

This revolutionizes our spiritual life: Instead of simply contenting ourselves with outward piety, or external religious observance, we begin to explore the depths of the God to whom we pray. As in the closest of human relationships, we are never satisfied knowing only the externals of the other but are drawn to know what makes him or her tick. The inner life of the beloved becomes a tender and bonding revelation, wherein we find ourselves spontaneously letting down our guard to meet the other in mutual vulnerability.

To underscore our need for perseverance along this inward journey, I sometimes begin retreats with an unusual but highly pertinent Scripture passage. When Jesus instructs his disciples in right conduct on their missions he, significantly, won't allow them to change their lodgings on a whim: "Whatever house you enter, first say, 'Peace be to this house!' ...And remain in the same house, eating and drinking what they provide...; do not go from house to house" (See: Lk 10:5–7).

Jesus' instructions apply naturally to religious life; stability in community life or perseverance in monastic work come most readily to mind. In fact, his words are a powerful antidote against our general human tendency to blame people or our environment when we lose inner peace. But going deeper than our living circumstances, community, or even family situation, there is a more important place of stability that we need to be anchored in—not a residential home, nor a monastery, nor any place of retreat. It is the soul. And it is that place above any other that the Lord calls his home.

This takes absolutely nothing away from our tabernacles and

monstrances, wherein our Lord is rightly adored and communed with. Yet as much as we surround the Blessed Sacrament with marks of honor and devotion, Jesus remains there so that he might ultimately live in our souls. Hence: "He who eats my flesh and drinks my blood abides in me, and I in him" (Jn 6:56).

It follows from this that both body and soul are elevated to sanctuary status:

> If a man loves me, he will keep my word, and my Father will love him, and we will come to him and make our home with him. (Jn 14:23)

> Do you not know that you are God's temple and that God's Spirit dwells in you? If anyone destroys God's temple, God will destroy him. For God's temple is holy, and that temple you are. (1 Cor 3:16–17)

> Do you not know that your body is a temple of the Holy Spirit within you, which you have from God? You are not your own; you were bought with a price. So glorify God in your body. (1 Cor 6:19–20)

As 'lord of the house and ruler of all its possessions' (See: Ps 105:20), God assumes a role beyond that of architect. As humble steward or servant, Jesus even assumes the role of "waiter" for those who, in prayerful vigilance, have waited on him:

> Let your loins be girded and your lamps burning, and be like

men who are waiting for their master to come home from the marriage feast, so that they may open to him at once when he comes and knocks. Blessed are those servants whom the master finds awake when he comes; truly, I say to you, he will gird himself and have them sit at table, and he will come and serve them. (Lk 12:35–37)

Outside of the house all is darkness, confusion, and hunger; within is something akin to the fiesta thrown for the prodigal son: music, merrymaking, dancing, and a choice meal. "My soul shall be filled" says the Psalms, "as with a banquet" (Ps 63:6).[2] This is because where the Lord lives and reigns, life and joy always flourish.

And the meal doesn't end there, but develops into a mystical table fellowship where both host and guest in some way nourish each other: "Behold, I stand at the door and knock; if any one hears my voice and opens the door, I will come in to him and eat with him, and he with me" (Rev 3:20). What fare we have to offer the Lord may seem too meager to mention, yet the Bible provides several hints. The Bridegroom of the Song of Solomon is said to pasture his flock "among the lilies" (2:16), while the same Bridegroom of the New Testament shares table fellowship with "tax collectors and sinners" (Lk 5:30). Those who are pure and innocent (the lilies) and those who know they are not, but want to be, this is the food that so delights Jesus, for it is the bread of our humility.

2   Revised Grail Psalter: https://www.giamusic.com/sacred_music/RGP/psalmDisplay.cfm?psalm_id=275,.

On our part, eating and drinking what is provided and resisting the urge to browse, to "snack" on foods of our own choosing, shows our appreciation of and fidelity to what the Lord of our house provides. Domestic analogies like this one ring true for all who have tried to pray with any kind of consistency. Whether it's the child reminded not to spoil his appetite or the working man waiting for dinner after a long day, the order from the kitchen is the same: wait. Van Zeller gives it a poetic turn: "The wilderness is strewn with souls who have not been content to wait."[3] Jumping the gun in the spiritual life, neglecting to wait on God, has always been the cause of lost vocations, lost opportunities to grow, and other aberrations in the life of prayer and ministry.

People often think they've gone wrong when their prayer begins to feel like nothing, or worse than nothing. A squandering of time and energy, a fruitless loneliness, a dream gone wrong—that's how the wilderness of prayer and perseverance seems. Or like being airdropped into some badlands, helplessly wandering without a survival kit. It is the Israelite journey to the promised land replayed over and over. The need to follow, to trust, to be content, will never not be necessary.

The moment it is most tempting to wander is precisely when it is most counterproductive to shuttle from house to house. We need to stay home with God within and let him provide a place of rest and nourishment.

3   Hubert van Zeller, *Spirituality Recharted*, p. 71.

It's no wonder that running away from home surges in our blood. Our first parents bequeathed to us an itch for more, even when we have everything. We are ever discontent with what we've got in hand, straining toward novelty, greener grass, the "distant country" that so allured the prodigal son. Having everything they could ask for in Eden, Adam and Eve yet allowed the tempter to goad them on for more, even god status. And since they enjoyed interior intimacy with God in paradise, their betrayal is all the more shocking and sobering for us, inheritors of their spiritual and moral handicaps.

In a roundabout way, I began to learn this lesson at the tender age of four or five. One morning I announced to my parents that I was going to run away from home. There comes a time in every boy's life, I thought, when he has to strike out on his own and see the world, and at kindergarten age I had decided my time had come. I think I even tied a small bundle to a stick, just to make it official.

I went out the front door and walked clear around the perimeter of the house (it wasn't even a large house) and ended up back at the front door. I went back inside. And that completed my adventure of running away from home. I think it lasted all of three minutes. I don't remember what was going through my mind during my mini-odyssey, but I think I saw pretty quickly that I really had nowhere to go. Nowhere to run away to.

Why am I telling you this in a chapter on the Holy Spirit? The idea of home, of finding God in our Christian lives, even of experiencing spousal union with the living God in our souls—this is really what the spiritual life is all about, and it is the Spirit that makes it happen.

Jesus has given us his Spirit so that he can be within us forever, not as an idle presence but a guiding one. St. Thomas Aquinas teaches that those closest to God are most disposed to respond to his promptings, to be docile to the "inward instinct of the Holy Spirit."[4] And this represents the full flowering of the Christian life.

If we're missing out on this uniquely symbiotic relationship, then we're probably feeling pretty lost or "homeless" much of the time. In commenting on mankind's general unhappiness, Blaise Pascal speaks in terms that apply directly to the interior life:

> The sole cause of man's unhappiness is that he does not know how to stay quietly in his room. A man wealthy enough for life's needs would never leave home … if he knew how to stay at home and enjoy it.[5]

We drift easily, get bored easily, get obsessed easily with people or things that could lead us away from the Lord. We spend a lot of time filling in the gap, tiding ourselves over, and meanwhile miss the meal that alone nourishes us, what St. John of the Cross beautifully calls the "supper that refreshes, and deepens love."[6]

To use an image from the prophets, we all have a well, a cistern, within us that is very dry. Perhaps it is even cracked, as Jeremiah says

4   See Thomas Aquinas, *Summa Theologaie* I-II, Q 68, a. 2, 3; *ST* III, Q 36, a. 5, resp.

5   Blaise Pascal, *Pensées*, no. 136/139. trans. A.J. Krailsheimer (London: Penguin Books, 1988), p. 67.

6   John of the Cross, *The Spiritual Canticle*, stanzas 14–15, in *The Collected Works of St. John of the Cross*, p. 525.

(See: Jer 2:13), and holds no water at all. We all have a place within that we have repeatedly tried to fill with things. We keep pouring something into a part of ourselves and as soon as we turn around, it's empty again. All attempts to find permanent contentment, peace, and fulfillment outside of God are doomed to fail, to leave us emptier than when we started.

But as in other cases of failure and disillusionment, this can also give birth to a search for a more meaningful and lasting solution.

Sometimes it takes a good dose of loneliness and restlessness, the bitterness of a betrayal, or some serious disappointment to create an inroad for this relationship, to awaken us to our need for it. Suffering is often the one and only thing that can catapult us from the realm of theory into the arena of experience, where we are forced to face issues we might otherwise sidestep. Friendship, closeness, and companionship are what we are made for, but even there, we can't stop on the surface, contenting ourselves with a close circle of companions and a few intimate friends. These we must have, but even they will never be enough to fill the void that God created for himself within our souls.

The moment we perceive our need for the love and communion that only the Spirit can bring, *the way in* has been opened. Or better, we have been opened to it. We want to rest in God at the center of our souls, in a repose like the best human love provides, but so different. Although all human closeness is necessarily temporary and imperfect, even tinged with disappointment, intimacy with the Lord ever deepens, is always fresh and renewing. We do not exhaust the source of life and love but become more fully immersed in it. Our inability to drink in the ocean, to count the stars of heaven or grains of sand on the seashore, are images of human limitation that tell the story of how our relationship with God grows. We are on a one-way journey where all that we gather along the way prepares us to receive an endless outpouring of divine love and communion, the beginnings of which are only tasted here below in our interior union with God.

However, lest we give the impression that this inner journey is undertaken only in sunshine and good weather, the way lined by singing birds and blooming meadows, a reality check is in order.

Jesus says that the way to life is narrow, and the interior life of spiritual growth falls within the constricted margins of this path. A narrow way, a narrow gate, means we must be lean to enter it: stripped of the superfluous, free from the lies we often tell ourselves and others in order to hide our true selves. We have to be real. The one who enters into a relationship with God cannot be a personality, an image, a fake of any kind. We are not just a name and social security number, a list of likes, a profile. Granted, most of us have so little self-knowledge when we come to God that we don't see the deeper things about ourselves right away, but we must be prepared to be uncovered one layer at a time. And at the same time God removes our outer layers, he reveals to us his inner life, clothing us instead with his very self: "...you have put off the old nature with its practices and have put on the new nature, which is being renewed in knowledge *after the image of its creator*" (Col 3:9–10).[7]

A bottomless descent where solitude is painfully felt, where it becomes almost tangible, is also the place where the most profound friendship is forged. For it is there, in silence, that we feel completely understood without our having explained a thing or uttered a single word. The Advocate and Counselor of our souls knows us, prays in us, intercedes for us, and fills our emptiness with his gentle presence. We stand naked before God, undisguised by vanity, vulnerable yet unafraid, wanting to know and be known in the simple humility of our being.

> Until now you had known that the Holy Spirit was dwelling in your soul, to sanctify it... But you hadn't really *grasped* this truth about his presence.
>
> Now you feel his Love within you, and you want to talk to him, to be his friend, to confide in him...[8]

Grasping this truth is the fruit of patiently staying at home, waiting on the Lord. It might mean sitting in an interior that is very plain, or very messy, or even in need of major repair and renovation, listening to the clock tick and the foundation settle as your background music. But it is God's house, the place where, however humble, his glory dwells (See: Ps 26:8)—and which he purchased at the greatest cost to himself.

7   Italics are the author's emphasis.
8   Josemaría Escrivá: *The Forge*, no. 430

Grasping this truth also helps us face a sharp criticism with which the Lord confronted the religious leaders of his time: The house can't simply *look* nice, with a pretty façade and neat interior. It must also be full of life, light, and love.

> Woe to you, scribes and Pharisees, hypocrites! for you are like whitewashed tombs, which outwardly appear beautiful, but within they are full of dead men's bones and all uncleanness. So you also outwardly appear righteous to men, but within you are full of hypocrisy and iniquity. (Mt 23:27–28)

As our Lord compares the human soul to a house, he also warns of its becoming the haunt of demons (See: Lk 11:24–26). Our soul, in other words, is never neutral, never multi-purpose, so to speak. Although the "empty, swept, and put in order" house into which the roving demon returns accompanied by a gaggle of cronies is made to be God's home, it can be repurposed if we leave it idle. The Lord never wants us only to sweep the house clean and leave it tidy but empty.

The most powerful example of a house completely cleansed and renewed comes from an old and familiar gospel friend and sister, St. Mary Magdalene. She was personally the house out of which Jesus had to exorcise a band of demons, seven in all (See: Lk 8:2). When Jesus found her, she was a wreck of a human being, haunted and trapped. Like many women, I would imagine, she was so burdened with shame that she never felt she could go forward in life, much less be beloved of God.

What rebuilding would it take for Jesus to show her the true beauty of her house? To get her to a point where she could say, with all humility and truth, "I have loved, O Lord, the beauty of thy house; and the place where thy glory dwelleth" (Ps 26:8)?[9]

The ancient tradition of St. Mary Magdalene having been a prostitute of some kind tells us much about how she must have seen herself. St. Paul's reminder that "you have been purchased, and at a price," helps us appreciate how she was used to being "purchased" at another price: a sum of money. How that would affect her self-appraisal is obvious: If being bought and sold, used and thrown away, was her daily experience, then her personal value was completely tied up with bargaining over what she could give, not who she was.

Along comes this Rabbi who has no interest in any of that. He looks at her and sees *her*. He looks at her and sees her goodness. He penetrates her probably rough exterior, gets beyond the cosmetics and jewelry, and sees one who is in desperate need of redemption, but first of all, of simple friendship.

The basic hunger of every human being is reflected here: We want others to recognize our genuine goodness. Not *the talents I have* or anything surface-level, but the goodness that *God himself has placed within me*. And God himself meets that need *with* himself: He comes to us and establishes his life within us so that should we ever wonder about our fundamental goodness, our lovability, he is there to field and defuse all doubts. "And by this we know that he abides in us, by

9   Douay-Rheims 1899 American Edition.

the Spirit which he has given us" (1 Jn 3:24).

When Jesus entered Mary Magdalene's life, he came as one who could pay her ransom with a price that would seal her (and our) dignity forever: "You know that you were ransomed from [your] futile ways…, not with perishable things such as silver or gold, but with the precious blood of Christ, like that of a lamb without blemish or spot" (1 Pt 1:18–19). St. Mary Magdalene really understood this by firsthand experience. And God wants us to have the same conviction: Seeing ourselves as a wreck, but that Jesus allowed himself to be destroyed so that *I* could be repaired. He entered the tomb for *my* sake and left it behind forever for *my* justification.

And Jesus doesn't stop at reconciling a fallen woman to God, doesn't simply send her away after exorcising her demons. He commissions this former sinner to announce the gospel of the Resurrection to his apostles. She is now trustworthy for going on mission for him, and credible because she has been transformed by him. "Go to my brethren and say to them, I am ascending to my Father and your Father, to my God and your God" (Jn 20:17). That's right: We sinners share the same God. The God of St. Mary Magdalene is my God too. The same Jesus who loved and saved her also loves and saves me.

Consider what fills your house: order, life, and love, or dead men's bones, clutter, corruption? Does the Spirit have liberty to move you freely or is he under guard?

All of us have tried to make something fit where there isn't enough room, trying to store or arrange things and getting frustrated because there isn't enough space. We are especially bothered when we want to keep everything, as we step back and wonder: *Can I somehow hold on to everything? Can I make it all fit without getting rid of anything?* For material things, personal possessions, supplies, the answer might be yes, or it might be no. It depends on how creative and resourceful you are. Spiritually, the answer is always no. You cannot have many masters, many lords. *You cannot serve both God and mammon.* One has to take precedence.

Our Lord suggests a potential crowd of things we may need to sort through when he says, "my word finds no place in you" (Jn 8:37). And since we often want to make everything fit, we juggle— experiencing all of the conflicts and tension that go along with juggling. There is only one thing necessary and we only have room for that. We don't have to make things fit, to crowd out one thing or another. We have to let go. We have to make room for God.

Since we often don't see clearly enough what needs to be done, nor have courage enough to carry out what we might see, we must let God the Holy Spirit sort through all of the incompatible clutter that we lug around, as he holds them up before us, asking, "Do you still want this? May I rid you of this now?" And each discard renders the soul that much lighter and simpler.

St. Augustine asks God to do the work not only of cleansing and repairing, but also of widening his constricted soul:

Too narrow is the house of my soul for you to enter into it:
let it be enlarged by you. It lies in ruins; build it up again. I

confess and I know it contains things that offend your eyes. Yet who will cleanse it? Or upon what other than you shall I call?[10]

In the end, the Spirit helps us not only to jettison this or that vice, but to do the great cleansing work for which he has been sent: to build us into Christ, to restore our dignity, the image of God in us often defaced by our sins. In him "the whole structure is joined together and grows into a holy temple in the Lord; in whom you also are built into it for a dwelling place of God in the Spirit" (Eph 2:21–22).

Finding the way home means finding the way into that temple. Why? Because no place can really be home for us unless we appraise our inner home as something more than a confused network of thoughts, feelings, appetites, and emotions. Knowing "the temple that we are" immediately clarifies our keep and discard list, our agenda, our hopes and loves. Instead of hacking through an inner jungle of frustrations and regrets, of misplaced desires and cynicism, we follow the Spirit's lead along a way we never would have discovered on our own, and which leads to the fullness of life.

In the most emphatic and heartfelt terms, Jesus assures us of an enduring intimacy with God that produces an immediate and personal knowledge of him—akin to sharing the same roof with a loved one:

And I will pray the Father, and he will give you another

10 Augustine, *Confessions*, Book 1.5, trans. John K. Ryan (Garden City, NY: Image Books, 1960), p. 46.

Counselor, to be with you forever, even the Spirit of truth, whom the world cannot receive, because it neither sees him nor knows him; you know him, for he dwells with you, and will be in you.

I will not leave you desolate; I will come to you. Yet a little while, and the world will see me no more, but you will see me; because I live, you will live also. In that day you will know that I am in my Father, and you in me, and I in you. (Jn 14:16–20)

Perhaps these promises don't strike modern people as powerfully as they ought to. If the sacrament of confirmation is not as valued today as it was in the early Church, maybe it is because our adoption is also too much overlooked. The intimate connection between them is brought out succinctly in the liturgical preface for the solemnity of Pentecost. Note how the sending of the Holy Spirit is no extra to the Christian life, but the fulfillment of Redemption in Christ:

For, bringing your Paschal Mystery to completion,
you bestowed the Holy Spirit today
on those you made your adopted children
by uniting them to your Only Begotten Son.
This same Spirit, as the Church came to birth,
opened to all peoples the knowledge of God
and brought together the many languages of the earth

in profession of the one faith.[11]

Confirmation has practically become a Catholic rite of passage, a type of graduation ceremony in which teenagers are asked to commit themselves publicly to their faith, to decide whether they're all in or not. But not only does this skew the purpose of the sacrament, it undermines the mission of the Holy Spirit in our lives. It implies that the Church is setting her seal upon our decisions, rather than anointing us with the grace to decide for Christ.

But perhaps even more unfortunate is the neglect of the friendship the Spirit brings. Failure to appreciate the gift of the Holy Spirit couldn't come at a worse time: when young people especially need to be assured of their own worth, of the closeness of a friend. They are often tempted turn away from the guarantee of both. They may not know what or whom they are receiving and so fail to appreciate what they're leaving behind.

Jesus wants us to enjoy his gifts of life, love, joy, and peace to the full because, as St. Josemaría reminds us, "The presence and the action of the Holy Spirit are a foretaste of eternal happiness, of the joy and peace for which we are destined by God."[12] Without that foretaste it is not at all easy to reach that eternal blessedness. Human beings need incentives to move forward and joy, peace, and love are the ones that move us more than anything else.

If we lack this promised joy and peace, the "foretaste of eternal

11 *Roman Missal*, 3rd ed.

12 Escrivá, *Christ is Passing By*, no. 130.

happiness," we really have only one place to look to find out why: *What's going on in my heart? Am I allowing the Spirit to be Lord of my heart, my interior life, my entire life?* If the earliest Christians had a deeper sense of God's work within the soul, it is not because such awareness was more automatic or effortless for them. In fact, it's not mainly a matter of effort at all. Listen to the simplicity of St. John's claim, "By this we know that we abide in him and he in us, because he has given us of his own Spirit" (1 Jn 4:13), or that of St. Paul citing the inspiration to call God "Abba, Father" as a sign of God's Spirit within. The implication is a calm attentiveness to the Lord within, a willingness to listen and respond, a contemplative gaze, not at self but at the divine movements within oneself.

The Spirit's work, depicted by St. Josemaria as "polishing, uprooting, and enkindling," creates a longing within us to keep commandments, to be faithful—both of which confirm our awareness of being loved and a wish to return that love through obedience. The clearest sign that we have grasped the truth of the Spirit's presence within is this personal accountability, this kinship, we feel in response to the Spirit's love: "You feel his Love within you, and you want to talk to him, to be his friend, to confide in him..."[13]

We often associate the Holy Spirit with the *extraordinary*: with miracles, signs, and wonders. And that is right, but incomplete. Because the same Spirit that produces signs and wonders through the hands of the apostles produces in every disciple something even

13 The Forge, no. 430.

more wonderful: the capacity to love like Christ, the strength to lay down our lives for others in the name of Christ. This is worth more than all miracles combined. Because the Holy Spirit's main work in us is to remake us into *other Christs*.

The Holy Spirit manifests himself by miracles on an 'as-needed' basis. But more often he acts in a quieter way. He simply enables us to love God and neighbor, to have confidence in God, to serve God "not only without a murmur, but even with delight."[14] Is there any miracle you would rather see instead of loving and serving God in your life with a confidence and joy that no one can take away from you? With a delight that can outshine any obstacle or difficulty?

St. Josemaria shows us the way to this:

Listen to him, I insist. He will give you strength. He will do everything, if you so want.

Pray to him: Divine Guest, Master, Light, Guide, Love, may I make you truly welcome inside me and listen to the lessons you teach me. Make me burn with eagerness for you, make me follow you and love you.[15]

---

14 Augustine, *On Christian Doctrine*, 1.15, *NPNF: First Series*, vol. 2, p. 526. This public domain work can be accessed at www.newadvent.org.

15 Josemaría Escrivá, *The Forge* (New York: Scepter, 2002), no. 430.

CHAPTER FOUR
The Way Out: The Eucharist

He is our bread, our source of living water who allays our hunger

and satisfies our thirst.

–ST. PAUL VI[1]

Rigging a chance meeting is a classic stratagem in the ways of courtship. Boy meets girl because boy plants himself in a place where girl will pass by—remarking with studied nonchalance on the happy coincidence of their both being in the same place at the same time. God is not above this tactic. In fact, he plays the game better than even the most ardent human lover.

A brief detour into first century Samaria, learning more of the backstory of the transformed woman mentioned in the last chapter, will provide a timeless and frankly gorgeous example of God's tender

1 Pope Paul VI, Homily given in Manila (November 29, 1970): https://w2.vatican.va/content/paul-vi/en/homilies/1970/documents/hf_p-vi_hom_19701129.html

and relentless ways. However, since all the ways of the Lord are mercy and truth (See: Tobit 3:2), none can really be a detour. In fact, what appears as a chance meeting between Jesus and an unrefined woman is actually an eternally planned *rendezvous*, orchestrated entirely by the mind and heart of God. Call it a divine courtship and you won't be far from the kingdom of God.

And if the goal of every courtship is the wedding day, what must God have on his mind here? Where is he leading her, leading us? To a feast known as the wedding supper of the Lamb.

"Hallelujah! For the Lord our God the Almighty reigns. Let us rejoice and exult and give him the glory, for the marriage of the Lamb has come, and his Bride has made herself ready; it was granted her to be clothed with fine linen, bright and pure"—for the fine linen is the righteous deeds of the saints.

And the angel said to me, "Write this: Blessed are those who are invited to the marriage supper of the Lamb." (Rev 19:6–9)

But Revelation's righteously-robed bride was not born thus outfitted. She needed to be saved, but first courted, then cleansed, and finally splendidly arrayed. From courtship to communion banquet— this is the entire trajectory of Christian life, and the destination of this humble conversation at a Samaritan watering hole. As we trace a path there, we will find an unexpectedly direct route to the Eucharist.

In this, as in so many other areas of our faith, St. Augustine shows how doctrine speaks directly to the human soul as he connects the hunger for love and the fulfillment the Eucharist alone can give:

> I had not yet fallen in love, but I was in love with the idea of it, and this feeling that something was missing made me despise myself for not being more anxious to satisfy the need. I began to look around for some object for my love, since I badly wanted to love something…. [A]lthough my real need was for you, my God, who are the food of the soul, I was not aware of this hunger. I felt no need for the food that does not perish, not because I had had my fill of it, but because the more I was starved of it the less palatable it seemed.[2]

Everything Augustine candidly says here about himself could come as spontaneously from the heart of the nameless woman of Samaria in retrospect, reflecting on what happened that day when Jesus showed up in her life.

Our Lord's seemingly casual stop for rest at the well of Sychar sets the stage for an encounter without parallel in the Gospels (Jn 4:1–42). As soon as Jesus sends the disciples into the Samaritan village to fetch provisions, a lone woman heads out to gather water from the well. And there she finds a stranger—alone, tired, and thirsty. This is her God waiting for her, and what a God he is to be so human, so delicate, even vulnerable with her. He declares both his thirst and inability to slake it without her help. But gradually her eyes are opened; the thirsty man seated before her is far less thirsty than she.

2   Augustine, *Confessions*, 3.1, trans. R.S. Pine-Coffin (London: Penguin Books, 1961), p. 55.

In the space of a conversation, the woman begins to recognize her true thirst, buried under the debris of short-term relationships. She needed men, relationships, in her life continually; at least that's what she thought. By the time she meets Jesus, she's had five "husbands," in addition to the one she's currently living with.

But so long as she lacks the one necessary relationship, namely, a close friendship with God, she will never make the right match. And at this point, no doubt, she's likely already abandoned any dream of finding a permanent companion. When she comes to the well she has one objective in mind only: to get her jar filled with water. She's not asking for the gift of God, living water, or anything else this strange Jew could give her. She had already found a way to handle her own problems. She was surviving.

But Jesus took a simple, everyday errand and turned it into a revelation. It wasn't until he opened up her private life that she began to understand what her choices *really* said about her and her thirst: "I know that you've been with 'x' number of men," he says in so many words. "I know that you're living with a man right now who isn't your husband. Can we talk about this?" For her sake and ours, we're grateful she didn't run away, but stayed there to hear what Jesus had to say.

In pop culture, following the serial relationships of celebrities is for many a pastime, a form of entertainment, a morbid curiosity—not what it often ought to be: a cause for pity and prayer. Those accustomed to taking multiple relationships for granted may not see what the problem is when hearing the story of the Samaritan woman periodically at Mass. But as we mentioned early on in these pages, retrospect enlightened by faith, by grace, reveals a narrative that many saints very bluntly recount as a fruitless search for the infinite among the most appealing (but finite) pleasures the world has to offer. Having found God on the other end, they see more clearly the vanity of their attempts. And, like Augustine, they lament the lost time and wasted energy.

But however misguided and self-defeating this woman's life is, in the end Jesus entrusts the most important truth about his identity to her, seldom shared so explicitly with any other: "I who speak to you am the Christ." And off she runs back into the village to proclaim the message, astonishing her fellow Samaritans. She who formerly hadn't been particularly religious is now preaching. As in the case of Mary Magdalene, Jesus commissions a fallen woman with extremely important information, and for the same reason: Both are credible witnesses to Jesus because now, amazingly, they are filled with a joy and hope that can only come from communion with God.

In the end, this divinely orchestrated meeting and conversation is an unassuming intervention from one whose abiding message is redemption and renewed life. We can hear Jesus saying: "I've watched you take this trip to the well countless times. I've seen your anxiety. I've seen your heartbreak. I've witnessed your despair. And I haven't been a spectator. I've been involved. And I have brought you to this moment, today, where you can leave behind your jar and come to me and drink."

This is a true story. Maybe it is your story too. Maybe you've also been lugging around an empty jar of your own for years and you're as thirsty as ever. But wherever you are, Jesus sees you as you are right now, and he loves you as much as he loved the Samaritan woman. And the same offers he makes to her, he likewise tenders to you. He not only wants to give you life-giving water, but also a food that will preserve your life forever.

Our side trip into Samaria is a prologue, a crucial prologue, to what the Church calls "the source and summit of the Christian life"[3]: the Eucharist. The Eucharist is the missing relationship that every human being needs to be fulfilled in this life and in the world to come. The Eucharist is Jesus, the same Jesus who sat tired at the well and evangelized a woman who was not at all happy to see him. She was confrontational and skeptical, but it was all a façade.

Jesus also continues to breach our façade in daily life, to touch our hearts where they are raw and needy, maybe even hardened, and certainly where they hunger and thirst most. But he doesn't always wait until we're kneeling in church to do so. He often meets us in the very places where we go to fill our empty jars, whatever that place might be for each of us. It might surprise us to learn that "Jesus, who has encouraged this feeling of emptiness in us, comes out to meet us."[4] It's all his doing, even to the point of taking the damage we've done to ourselves and using its wreckage as the material for dialogue and conversation. If we learn nothing else from John 4, we certainly learn that.

3   *Catechism of the Catholic Church*, 1324.
4   Escrivá, *Christ is Passing By*, no. 170.

Newman describes where the Lord finds us and in what condition he finds us, in words that sketch the profile of our anonymous Samaritan:

Here then Christ finds us, weary of that world in which we are obliged to live and act, whether as willing or unwilling slaves to it. He finds us needing and seeking a home, and making one, as we best may, by means of the creature, since it is all we can do. The world, in which our duties lie, is as waste as the wilderness, as restless and turbulent as the ocean, as inconstant as the wind and weather. It has no substance in it, but is like a shade or phantom; when you pursue it, when you try to grasp it, it escapes from you, or it is malicious, and does you a mischief. We need something which the world cannot give: this is what we need, and this it is which the Gospel has supplied.[5]

We're doing our best in the world to make it our home, our happiness, our fulfillment. But it is not merely melancholic or pessimistic to declare all these efforts stillborn. They succeed only partially, and were never meant to do more. Although God speaks in the beautiful things of nature, most of us still require a dose of bitterness and disappointment before we will yearn to taste and see how good the Lord is. To meet our deepest needs, needs that we may not be able to identify all at once, Jesus ultimately wants to draw us into his Eucharistic presence: to the Mass, to the monstrance, to the

5   John Henry Newman, "The Church a Home for the Lonely," in *Parochial and Plain Sermons*, vol. 4 (London: Longmans, Green, and Co., 1897), pp. 189–90.

tabernacle. If we're not yet hungry and thirsty enough, Jesus will use the circumstances of lives to increase both.

Another true story of buried longing for God features a young man whose loneliness was cured by a priest's simple reminder during a Sunday homily: "With Jesus always present in the tabernacle, we never have a reason to feel lonely."[6] But the reason it so resonated with him was due to disappointment in love. He had started attending that particular parish to cross paths with a girl whom he knew attended Mass there. The hoped-for encounter never actually happened. What did happen, though, was a totally unexpected encounter with the Lord.

Continuing to attend Mass at the young lady's home parish, he soon heard the homily that stirred his desire for a more lasting relationship, a more permanent resolution to his problem. Although he had kind of suspected that the girl wasn't the main issue anyway, he couldn't give a name to his need. In the end, God used one love to draw the boy upward into another love: from the romantic to the divine. Finally, the young man discovered the abiding joy of the Eucharistic holy hour and began spending an hour a day before the Blessed Sacrament. He had found the love he had really been seeking all along.

6   Worth quoting here are a few lines from a letter of the Venerable Mother Luisa Josefa of the Most Blessed Sacrament (1866–1937): "Don't feel alone because you're not. Our Lord in the Blessed Sacrament wants to be your Confidant, your Friend, your Consoler. He wants to fill your soul with His love. Perhaps that's why He is making you feel the emptiness of creatures…. He wants you all for Himself" (Letter 318). *In Love's Safekeeping: The Letters and Spiritual Writings of Mother Maria Luisa Josefa of the Most Blessed Sacrament, OCD,* vol. 2, trans. Basil Frison, CMF, and Maria de la Paz Ayon, OCD, Carmelite Sisters of the Most Sacred Heart of Los Angeles, 1999, p. 532.

God goes fishing with a hook baited according to our tastes, to lead us to the bread that satisfies every taste (See: Wis 16:20). Not surprisingly, the heart's hunger for love is the desire we're most driven to follow. St. Cyril of Jerusalem (313–386) in his famous catechetical lectures to recent converts confirms that people haven't changed from the early centuries until now. God is not at all put off by those who initially come to the Church for less than supernatural motives. Truth be told, God is also behind those lesser motives.

> Perhaps you have come with a different motive: perhaps you are courting, and a girl is your reason—or, conversely, a boy. Many a time, too, a slave has wished to please his master, or a friend his friend. I allow the bait, and I welcome you in the trust that, however unsatisfactory the motive that has brought you, your good hope will soon save you. Maybe you did not know where you were going, or what sort of net it was in which you were to be caught. You are a fish caught in the net of the Church. Let yourself be taken alive: don't try to escape. It is Jesus who is playing you on His line, not to kill you, but, by killing you, to make you alive.[7]

It took a pretty girl to get our young man into the door of that parish church. It took a broken heart to put him on his knees before the tabernacle. Jesus took both, used both, and brought him a fulfillment

7   Cyril of Jerusalem, "The Introductory Lecture," in *The Works of Saint Cyril of Jerusalem*, vol. 1: (*Protocatechesis*), in *The Fathers of the Church*, trans. Leo P. McCauley and Anthony A. Stephenson (Washington, D. C.: CUA Press, 1969), pp. 74–75.

he didn't know how to ask for, not having known the true meaning of his hunger and thirst. Now, he was not only being fed. He was home.

Sometimes we need to be reminded of the obvious, and perhaps it takes a particularly difficult moment for a familiar truth to hit home: Jesus is "here on earth for you."[8] The Lord does not remain with us in the Eucharist for his own sake, but to meet our deepest human needs for love and friendship:

> Our Lord Jesus Christ, as though all the other proofs of his mercy were insufficient, institutes the Eucharist so that he can always be close to us. We can only understand up to a point that he does so because Love moves him, who needs nothing, not to want to be separated from us.[9]

In some, like that young man, the Lord allows a particularly distressing loneliness so that they will seek him out and discover the truth of another equally simple reminder: "When you approach the Tabernacle remember that he has been awaiting you for twenty centuries."[10]

The Eucharist penetrates to the heart of the human problem: "No one, man nor woman, can stand alone; we are so constituted by nature; and the world, instead of helping us, is an open adversary. It but increases our solitariness."[11] St. John Henry Newman portrays

8   Josemaría Escrivá, *The Way* (New York: Scepter, 2002), no. 539.

9   Escrivá, *Christ is Passing By*, no. 84.

10 Josemaría Escrivá, *The Way* (New York: Scepter, 2002), no. 537.

11 Newman, "The Church a Home for The Lonely," p. 196.

here an 'unsolvable' dilemma: God has made us to seek communion with others, yet everywhere we turn, everyone and everything falls short. The world can offer no lasting remedy.

We are all born with a radical loneliness that nothing can finally cure except a close communion with the Lord. Adam and Eve lost not only original innocence, but also the continual sense of God dwelling with and within them. Close human relationships are indispensable, but even their comfort can't reach our deeper, inherited solitude. Those deeper places within us are God's domain, and he reserves the power to touch those depths to himself alone.

This is why Jesus doesn't have to explain why an *abiding* relationship with him is desirable. We get the point as soon as we hear it. The Lord doesn't need to explain why we seek friendship, love, union with others. As our Creator, he has made us this way; we're "hardwired" not only to want God, but to have him abide with us always. It's a gospel pattern: Those who have been touched by the Lord—by his words or by a healing—often beg to accompany him, or beg him to stay with them.

Our Lord's express desires for union with us are both marvelous and mysterious, yet they make perfect sense to those tuned in to their own need for love—that is, those who have learned the difference between the transitory and shallow relationships and the only one that *abides*. How can we settle for less? For those who find the answer to the mystery of their own hunger and thirst in Jesus, the Eucharist is no mystery. Love makes perfect sense of it. Jesus promises this mutual abiding and we *get it*. We recognize it as what we've always wanted.

Think of the human experience of two people who love each other, and yet are forced to part. They would like to stay together forever, but duty—in one form or another—forces them to separate. They are unable to fulfil their desire of remaining close to each other, so man's love—which, great as it may be, is limited—seeks a symbolic gesture. People who make their farewells exchange gifts or perhaps a photograph with a dedication so ardent that it seems almost enough to burn that piece of paper. They can do no more, because a creature's power is not so great as its desire.

What we cannot do, our Lord is able to do. Jesus Christ, perfect God and perfect man, leaves us, not a symbol, but a reality. He himself stays with us.[12]

Yet many who heard the first announcement of the Eucharist reacted against it: "'This is a hard saying; who can listen to it?'" soon followed by the sad commentary, "After this many of his disciples drew back and no longer went about with him" (Jn 6:60, 66). It's not that they lacked intelligence. They may not have been entirely clear on the meaning of our Lord's words, but one thing *was* clear: Jesus was asking a very personal involvement that seemed to go too far. And everyone knows that love, real love, is what this involvement meant. They didn't want something so demanding, so personal, as this relationship would have to be: "He who eats my flesh and drinks

12 Escrivá, *Christ is Passing By*, no. 83.

my blood abides in me, and I in him. As the living Father sent me, and I live because of the Father, so he who eats me will live because of me" (Jn 6:56–7).

The people are not willing to cross the line between being interested in Christ and being totally involved with him. And so they return to their former way of life where the demands of this relationship are not going to complicate their lives and compromise their plans. They go back to where the demands of the Gospel are absent. They go back to an "easier" way. Perhaps it is an easier way, but life without Christ and his Gospel also makes one feel trapped in this world, a prisoner of appetites and desires that nothing can satisfy. They will be hungry always in their prison.

And by giving us himself as the Bread of Life, Jesus is all but shouting to us: *The Eucharist is the only way out!* This bread and this wine satisfy every taste because they feed the hunger and thirst of the spirit. No human formula, recipe, or magic spell could ever come close to doing what the Eucharist does for the heart that enters into this vital communion with Jesus. Nothing has ever succeeded in supplying the deepest needs of the soul like the Bread of Life.

When Christ enters our unredeemed lives, he finds us adrift: searching, sinning, mistaking good for evil and evil for good; looking for love, friendship, some connection with others that will make us whole. But if we are open to his gentle invitations and promptings, this is also how we may find God: as incomplete (perhaps lonely) people needing to be taken in and sheltered from our confused search.

All of mankind needs "some shelter, refuge, rest, home, or

sanctuary from the outward world," as Newman characterizes our situation, and this very drive can lead people to discover the "shelter or secret place which God has provided for them in Christ."[13] In the Eucharist, Jesus Christ himself becomes our shelter, our place of refuge.

"Lord, to whom shall we go? You have the words of eternal life; and we have believed, and have come to know, that you are the Holy One of God" (Jn 6:68–69). As the people left in droves from the synagogue at Capernaum, unwilling to accept the teaching on the Eucharist, St. Peter avowed that he and the apostles would not abandon him. He speaks on our behalf, and on behalf of all who have had this deep contact with the Lord, saying in effect: *We've already had enough personal contact with you, Lord, to know that going back to our former lives means stranding ourselves again on the very shoreline where You found us. We know that there is no place else to go.*

Jesus is our home, our refuge in this world, as we look forward to the glorious promise of the next: "And he who sits upon the throne will shelter them with his presence" (Rev 7:15).

---

13 Newman, "The Church a Home for the Lonely," p. 187.

CHAPTER FIVE
To Be Loved by a Sacred Heart

We ought to meditate most lovingly on the beating of His Sacred Heart...
After the Redeemer, conqueror of death, rose from the dead, His most Sacred
Heart never ceased, and never will cease, to beat...

–VENERABLE POPE PIUS XII[1]

n an earlier chapter God's merciful love was identified as the connecting thread that, in ways known mostly to God alone, unites everything in our lives. Our ignorance as to how all things work together is a concession we might make with some anxiety, but always without apology, because faith in God assures us that they do. And without faith we can't even approach God, much less be pleasing to him (See: Heb 11:6). In spite of the human capacity for choosing both very good and very wicked things, the fact remains: Whether we see convergence or only contradiction, God is using all things in this world for good, for glory.

As soon as you accept "God is love" (1 Jn 4:8) not only as who

God is but what he does, then allowing its practical consequence is inevitable: that God ultimately acts only out of love. In a fallen world, however, God's love will frequently look very obscure to us; as it carefully picks through the rubble of destructive human choices, it yet crowns the spires of the noblest aspirations. Hubert van Zeller, in his characteristically incisive and matter-of-fact style, puts it like this:

> We see the hand of God, infinitely patient, working out his will through what appears to be labyrinthine chaos. How else account for history's catalog of cruelties, blunders, unfairness, infidelity? There must be love behind it all or he would have brought the whole thing to an end long ago.[2]

To take the greatest example as the norm: Most of those who stood on the sidelines of the Lord's passion, not to mention those humanly responsible for it, had divine love least of all on their minds. Yet in laying down his life for the life of the world God was loving the world in the greatest and most exhaustive way possible. Many didn't care; some laughed; others thought "good riddance." The ones who followed and wept, who consoled and reverenced Jesus, still felt defeated at the end of the day. And that was the mixed review of the passion of Jesus Christ. So does God's love continue to get mixed reviews, and mostly from the same kinds of critics who lack the perception and discernment born of faith to know what God is doing. At some point, heaven knows, all of us have been such critics.

2   Hubert van Zeller, *Spirituality Recharted*, p. 86

It should come as no surprise that if our lives and all of world history are explainable by love or mercy, then much more is the life of Jesus, the author of both. Commenting on Ezekiel 18:23, St. Josemaría writes:

"Have I any pleasure in the death of the wicked, says the Lord God, and not rather that he should turn from his way and live?" These words explain Christ's whole life. They allow us to understand why he has come to us with a heart made of flesh, a heart like ours. This is a convincing proof of his love and a constant witness to the mystery of divine charity.[3]

It takes very little experience of our human weakness to understand why God would come to us bearing a true human heart. He is the first one to tell us how perplexing, "unsearchable," and even "perverse" it can be (See: Jer 17:9). But he is also the first one to reach out to us in love, loving us before we even desire his love or know how to ask for it, much less return it. When we feel ourselves broken and unlovable, we find the Lord going before us to cushion our despondency on the pillow of his breast. Clearly, we need not only contact but *communion* with a heart that, although unsearchable because it is infinite, is certainly not shy about searching our hearts and uncovering both the bad and the good that we didn't know were there.

Only the outreach of a heart greater than our own can effect lasting

3   Escrivá, *Christ is Passing By, no. 162.*

change in us. "The heart is commonly reached," writes Newman,

> not through the reason, but through the imagination, by
> means of direct impressions, by the testimony of facts and
> events, by history, by description. Persons influence us, voices
> melt us, looks subdue us, deeds inflame us.[4]

And this is exactly what Jesus does for us in walking "our" earth, speaking our language, eating our food, loving with the very heart he had made specifically for us to love with. His humanity—face, voice, and gestures—all capture the heart, and were made to do so.

God can say "I love you" from heaven, as someone might write it to a friend. But until that love comes robed in flesh like ours, it might seem too distant, even detached and abstract, for us to cling to. Newman's famous motto as Cardinal *Cor ad cor loquitur* ("Heart speaks to heart") makes the point: The heart of God speaks to us directly, in a wholly *other* and completely perfect way, while continuing to beat as humanly and rhythmically as any man's heart does. The communication between his heart and ours, in other words, is not like a nuclear physicist trying to explain atomic particles to a stone. It's not a matter of two disparate beings trying to find common ground. God has levelled the playing field by the Incarnation; he has DNA, fingerprints, measurable vital signs, a beating heart.

The tenderness and vulnerability of the heart are both its glory

---

4   John Henry Newman, "Secular Knowledge Not a Principle of Action," in *Discussions and Arguments on Various Subjects* (London: Longmans, Green, and Co., 1899), p. 293.

and agony. The depths of love and communion of which the heart is capable finds counterbalance in the capacity for deep and lasting hurt. "Any wound," moans Sirach, "but not a wound of the heart!" (Sir 25:13). Hence our need for a heart whose love we need never question or fear, in which absolutely no self-interest or exploitation holds sway, no shadows of manipulation, no hidden agenda, and no possibility of vacillation or failure.

By the time we reach adulthood we've been loved by any number of hearts, with more or less success, and with some damage inflicted along the way. We know how it feels to be used or taken advantage of, betrayed, or simply disappointed by someone. It puts us on guard ever after, and normally damages our ability to trust. We also know what it is to be loved by honest-to-goodness fallen people—by people who sincerely try, yet fail to love well. We know our own failures in this area acutely.

One heart alone among all who have or do love us is unfailing, all-knowing, supplying every need; one alone knows all of the circumstances of our choices, the excusing factors that sometimes mitigate our sins; one alone knows how we ended up the way we are and what we need to become who we ought to be. This heart knows our way home. This heart, in fact, is our home.[5] And this one we

5   St. Josemaría beautifully elaborates this point, identifying the heart of Christ as, paradoxically, both the place where we live fulfilled as human beings and where God in turn makes our hearts his home: "Living in Christ's heart, being closely united to him means, therefore, that we become a dwelling place of God. 'He who loves me, my Father will also love,' our Lord told us. And Christ and the Father in the Holy Spirit come to the soul and make their home there." (*Christ is Passing By*, no. 170.)

call *sacred*.

All people want a heart to love them—and not just any heart, but the perfect heart. The perfect heart to love imperfect 'me' in a perfect way. And when we see the Sacred Heart with its iconic features of fire, thorns, and blood, we say: *That's it! That's what I've been looking for my whole life, a heart just like that. You don't need to explain the thorns, the fire, the cross that sits on top. It all speaks to me. I get it. That's the kind of love that I was made for.* Whenever we see the Sacred Heart we understand it because we feel immediately understood by it. And this is true whether we count ourselves among the most innocent or the most guilty of sinners.

Jesus knows that we need the love of a crucified heart, a heart on fire, a heart that suffers and bleeds, and asks for no repayment except our love in return. That's why when we see the Sacred Heart, we get it. Nobody needs to stand there like a museum docent and explain its attributes. We get it, because it's what we've always wanted, because God has created us to want it more than anything else.

This explains how, if God sometimes wounds our hearts or at least permits them to ache, it is never retaliation or spite. "For he wounds," says Job, "but he binds up; he smites, but his hands heal" (Jb 5:18). Wounding, in other words, is often the result of love—a touch that tenderly bruises where we are most sensitive. God's healing touch, like a physician's remedy, often stings not because the healer is rough but because the area is tender to the touch.

St. John of the Cross records this feeling with greater intensity and delicacy than almost anyone, often speaking of a wound of love that simultaneously tortures and delights. After begging in the "Spiritual Canticle," "Why, since you wounded this heart, don't you heal it?"[6] he goes on in "The Living Flame of Love" to exult in the vulnerability created in the soul by the finger of God:

> O living flame of love
> that tenderly wounds my soul
> in its deepest center!...
> O sweet cautery,
> O delightful wound!
> O gentle hand! O delicate touch...[7]

Although the language borrows from the romantic, evoking human passion, make no mistake: God is the flame that burns so intimately, consuming without destroying, and he alone has the power to sear the soul that deeply and sweetly.

The heart is at its communicative best when it opens itself completely to another, empties its contents, and demonstrates vulnerability and trust. The Scriptural injunction "pour out your heart before him" (Ps 62:8) is marvelously reciprocated by God in Christ. As we have seen, Jesus especially pours out his heart at the Last Supper, expressing deep, heartfelt desire for communion with us—not out of any neediness, but out of pure love. But the

6   John of the Cross, *The Spiritual Canticle*, stanza 9, in *The Collected Works of Saint John of the Cross*, p. 472.

7   John of the Cross, *The Living Flame of Love*, stanzas 1–2, in *The Collected Works of Saint John of the Cross*, p. 52.

outpouring does not end there. Jesus still speaks in the depths of our souls—from the Lord's encouragement to St. Paul to continue speaking boldly (See: Acts 18:9), to the many saints and mystics who, throughout the centuries, have recorded the most extraordinary exchanges between the Lord and themselves. One need only page through the twentieth-century *Diary* of St. Faustina Kowalska to see dialogues of the rarest beauty.

This prepares us to explore now what it means for us to be loved by the Sacred Heart, today, in our lifetime. Reading about how God has loved other people and drawing inspiration from that is important. But if it stops there, without translation into our ordinary lives, we slip into museum mode: admiring beautiful exhibits, but at a safe distance. With the Lord there is no safe distance. His handiwork, the saints, shows us in an uncompromising way what he wants his love to do for us: to renew, rebuild, beautify what has perhaps fallen to pieces, been vandalized, or simply neglected.

You can tell from Scripture that God generally regards us as a fatigued, thirsting, helpless race; lost sheep and broken cisterns are among the Biblical descriptions of our waywardness. And yet the same Lord urges us to embrace a mystery about ourselves: We are capable of receiving and giving the greatest possible love. He sees in us a capacity that we may not even see in ourselves, and not simply because he is all-seeing. As we mentioned earlier, he has hollowed out our core to house himself alone. We are not only the sheep of his pasture, but we are his pasture as well.

The Lord's parable of the shepherd who goes out into the

wilderness in search of the one astray, leaving the ninety-nine behind, seems to presage an arduous quest capped by a scolding when he finds it (Lk 15:1–7). But what does he do in fact? No dressing down, no reproaches. Instead, Jesus says he puts the sheep on his shoulders—*rejoicing, rejoicing, rejoicing.* What is that supposed to do for your soul when you hear it? To recognize the joy that Jesus experiences in seeking us as we are, wherever we are, whoever we are, and drawing us close to his heart?

Listen to the effect it has on St. Bernard of Clairvaux (1090–1153). And remember, in the household of God he is a father and brother, not a distant historical personage. You are related to him in Christ.

> Nor can I fear to look on his face, since I have sensed his tenderness. In what have I known it? In this—not only has he sought me as I am, but he has shown me tenderness, and caused me to seek him with confidence. How can I not respond to him when he seeks me? … How can he be angry with me for seeking him, when he overlooked the contempt I showed for him? He will not drive away someone who seeks him, when he sought someone who spurned him. The spirit of the Word is gentle, and brings me gentle greetings, speaking to me persuasively of the zeal and desire of the Word, which cannot be hidden from him. He searches the deep things of God, and knows his thoughts—thoughts of peace & not of vengeance. How can I fail to be inspired to seek him, when I

have experienced his mercy and been assured of his peace?[8]

The effect of being sought after—whether by the Lord or by someone whom we love, especially when we feel ashamed and unworthy—is always the same: It fires us to seek the lover in return. To know that you are loved when you feel unlovable, when you have genuinely proved yourself weak, untrustworthy, and even traitorous, is the scandal of Christianity replayed in the life of every sinner. And the love is never neutral and passive, condoning vices, blessing excesses, endorsing disorders. If we learn nothing else from the New Testament, we learn that Jesus does not leave us as he found us, that his grace is squarely aimed at changing, renewing, transforming us into children of God and coheirs with Christ himself, our Brother.

This is the Shepherd's parable, but Jesus takes it one step further. He even claims that there is greater joy in heaven over one sinner who repents than over ninety-nine who don't need it so much. Think of that. The retrieval of a single missing sheep unbridles his heart's delight, and that of the heavenly hosts. Sometimes when I hear confessions I wish I could hear the angels sing, because they do. Why do they rejoice? Because every time repentance and conversion happen, the Sacred Heart has triumphed again. If you're going to rejoice over anything, rejoice over that: the victory of God's love in a person's life.

The image of Jesus gesturing meekly to his Sacred Heart loudly proclaims that we are made to receive a love that he describes as 'no

8   Bernard of Clairvaux, *Sermons on the Song of Songs*, vol. 4 (Kalamazoo, Mich.: Cistercian Publications, 1971), pp. 192-3.

greater.' Everywhere we turn in the liturgy for the solemnity of the Most Sacred Heart of Jesus, images of outpourings, of nourishment, of drawing water from its source meet us—all designed to reveal how that flaming, pierced, cross-surmounted Heart loves us. By his modest gesture, Jesus yet declares the ardor of his love: *I want you to want this. This is for you: the fire is for you, the cross is for you, the blood is for you, the thorns are for you. Take your rest here. This is where love comes from, where the grace and mercy flow from.*

Somehow we have to put contraries together: fire and water, pain and repose, sacrifice and refreshment. But there is no tension. Because Jesus comes to us "with a heart made of flesh, a heart like ours," seeming opposites smoothly dovetail. We know what it is to hunger and thirst for love as well as to burn with it. We know heartfelt restlessness and wholehearted repose. We know emptiness and fulfillment. What this means in God's heart is something that only he can tell us.

And Jesus does tell us. But less with words than with a single fact.

The perforation of his heart on Calvary, kept open for all to approach and receive, is that fact. Once the heart of Jesus was opened on Calvary, he never closed it again. It is still *hanging* open. This Physician did not heal himself: not in Heart, not in hands, not in feet, not in his side. It is essentially a crude stab wound, but it "speaks more graciously" even than the battered body of the righteous Abel (See: Heb 12:24). "Jesus allowed His side to be opened," writes St. Teresa Benedicta of the Cross (Edith Stein), "to show us that He opens His heart for us. It is presented to us as a place for us to reside."[9] Indeed, she continues, "complete consecration to the Divine Heart is reached only when He is our home, our daily residence, and center of our lives—when His life has become our life."[10]

The beautiful opening prayer for the Solemnity of the Most Sacred Heart of Jesus speaks of Christ's heart containing "boundless treasures" of love. The Sacred Heart is always open, always outpouring. Here, the title of Pius XII's encyclical on devotion to the Sacred Heart needs reiterating within its biblical context: "*Haurietis aquas* in gaudio de fontibus salvatoris" is "You shall draw waters with joy out of the Savior's fountain" (Is 12:3).[11]

We approach the heart of Jesus according to how much we recognize our need for his pasturing, our need for him to lead us "beside still waters" where he can restore our souls (Ps 23:2–3). The disoriented and stranded sheep of the Gospel was certainly disillusioned about his abilities and strengths. If he thought he could survive on his own, or just inattentively drift, finding himself deserted should have cured him of roving ever again. In any case, his sense of need for rescue was heightened by the unwanted solitude of loneliness. The Good Shepherd comes to save him, and the sheep

---

9   Edith Stein, "Das Herz Jesu—Unsere Wohnung" as quoted in M. Regina Van den Berg, *Communion with Christ: According to Saint Teresa Benedicta of the Cross* (San Francisco: Ignatius Press, 2015), p. 56.

10   Stein, "Eucharistische Erziehung,"as quoted in *Communion with Christ*, pp. 55–6.

11   Pius XII, Encylical on Devotion to the Sacred Heart *Haurietis Aquas* (May 15, 1956), 1. http://w2.vatican.va/content/pius-xii/en/encyclicals/documents/hf_p-xii_enc_15051956_haurietis-aquas.html.

is relieved to be carried home to safety.

Could it be that God so loves us that he will even permit some to stray, to feel adrift, in order to drive home our need for him? The Shepherd's goal is to get us on his shoulders where he can do the carrying, and we the receiving of his rest. Whether the initial draw comes from a positive desire for perfection or from the desperate need for a bailout, the Lord intends one thing: the joining of our hearts to his.

Some initially approach Jesus for one need that ends up being only the tip of the iceberg. A symptom can conceal a deeper problem that only the divine physician can identify and remedy. Some go to him because they are lonely and heartbroken. They want companionship, and Jesus stands above all hurt, pointing to his Heart, ringed with thorns, bleeding, supporting a cross and flames of love. *Finally*, the lonely soul has found One who understands everything. The Heart that loves and suffers like that One must be a Sacred Heart.

Others run to the Heart of Jesus because their lives are falling apart, or an area of life has become unmanageable. They need strength to stand against their bad habits, addictions, tormenting thoughts and feelings. Once again, Jesus rises above every other solution, gesturing silently to his Sacred Heart. *Finally*, the troubled soul has found him who once said to another struggling sinner: "My grace is sufficient for you, for my power is made perfect in weakness" (2 Cor 12:9).

Whether we identify with St. Paul's struggle or that of St. Mary Magdalene, the Samaritan woman, or some other lost-and-found soul, the riches of love contained in the Sacred Heart pay every price of every debt we've ever racked up, ransom us from futile and destructive ways, and open an expansive horizon before us where all of our human notions of love and fulfillment shrink to insignificance. As the Venerable Mother Luisita Josefa (1866–1937) was fond of saying, "You were born for greater things." And within the heart of Jesus is where those greater things are discovered.

> May Divine Love consume your soul! After all, that's the reason why we are in the world. All of the rest is nothing but a puff of smoke.[12]

---

12 Letter 118 in *In Love's Safekeeping: The Letters and Spiritual Writings of Mother Maria Luisa Josefa of the Most Blessed Sacrament, OCD,* vol. 1, trans. Basil Frison, CMF, and Maria de la Paz Ayon, OCD (Los Angeles: Carmelite Sisters of the Most Sacred Heart of Los Angeles, 1999), p. 217.

CHAPTER SIX
When Jesus Kneels Before Us: Reconciliation

When he had washed their feet, and taken his garments, and resumed his place, he said to them, "Do you know what I have done to you?"

–JOHN 13:12

S ome years ago I had the privilege of performing a wedding for a very devout and zealous couple. The beautiful wedding Mass featured Gregorian chant and polyphony, and the reception had everything you would expect: a festive banquet, music, and dancing—a joyful celebration.

But something happened at the reception that I don't think anyone was expecting. At a certain point, the music and dancing came to a halt. The dance floor was cleared. Out came the bridegroom, who set up a chair in the middle of the floor. After seating his bride in the chair, he proceeded to remove his tuxedo jacket and bring over a pitcher of water and a basin. Getting down on his hands and knees, he removed the bride's slippers and washed her feet, reenacting the *mandatum* for her, the ceremonial washing of the feet typically performed by priests on Holy Thursday, commemorating the Lord's washing of the apostles' feet (See: Jn 13:1–20).

Some wedding customs are sentimental, others tacky, still others are deliberately playful or silly. This one was inspired: "You also ought to wash one another's feet. For I have given you an example, that you also should do as I have done to you" (Jn 13:14–15). The bride will never forget what the bridegroom did for her on the day they were wedded, nor will he forget. The unexpected, poignant gesture at just the right moment leaves a lasting impression.

An unconventional overturning of accepted roles and postures is not always an act of rebellion or iconoclasm. Nor is it done only for the sake of romance. A theme we have often returned to in these pages appears again here: Once God enters our world as a man, everything is turned upside down, spiritually speaking. Once God empties himself, making himself the lowest of the low for our sake, then love looks radically different than before the Word became flesh. It humbles itself not to score points, but to love more fully, to complete the gift of self. And that is what our new husband was aiming at on the dance floor with his new wife: to make one of his first acts of love an act of imitation, reproducing the gestures of the Master to set the tone for their married life.

When Jesus undertakes the washing of his disciples' feet, his servant posture teaches us more than a theoretical or theological truth. That the Son of God possesses an infinite humility that he is not afraid to act on is the truth. But this posture speaks practically to the mess that our lives so easily become. The cleaning of the disciples' feet is the sign of a personal cleansing that Jesus alone can do for us. Even though we commonly (and rightly enough) talk about "forgiving" ourselves, we can really only do so if we know the cleansing forgiveness of Jesus Christ. If he can forgive each and every one of our trespasses, then we are emboldened to let the chains fall from our wrists and go free.

We need to see our sinful choices, regrets, failures, sorrow over life's misfortunes—everything that makes life painful and burdensome—as the stains that cling to our feet. If sometimes we feel humiliated by our wrong turns, then we need to see Jesus loving us as a servant. We cannot fall so far or so fast that Jesus can't get beneath us to catch us.

Jesus loves in a way that honors the dignity of the other or, if dignity has been lost, restores it. And he does this by abasing himself. At its best, love totally forgets its own dignity, its own everything, and launches itself into self-donation, somewhat like King David dancing before the Ark of the Covenant, heedless of his own royal stature. And to one who criticized his abandon with, "How the king of Israel honored himself today!," he countered without apology: "I will make myself yet more contemptible than this, and I will be abased in your eyes" (See: 2 Sam 6:20, 22).

Following Jesus' deliberate movements in the middle of the Passover meal, we are called to contemplate a sequence of uncomplicated gestures, made extraordinary by the one who enacts them, yet without "playacting." The Lord is dead serious about this. His heart is in it to an infinite degree. A servant tending to guests is normally an unobtrusive and forgettable presence. But as St. John prepares to recount the scene in his Gospel, he speaks with a solemnity that leaves no doubt about the import and sincerity of what we are about to witness:

> Now before the feast of the Passover, when Jesus knew that his hour had come to depart out of this world to the Father, having loved his own who were in the world, he loved them to the end. (Jn 13:1)

And for Jesus *loving his own unto the end* means not letting up in his self-sacrifice, not thinking twice about his own stature, and getting us to do the same:

> You call me Teacher and Lord; and you are right, for so I am. If I then, your Lord and Teacher, have washed your feet, you also ought to wash one another's feet. For I have given you an example, that you also should do as I have done to you. (Jn 13:13–15).

He says much the same thing in his critique of Gentile ways, also fittingly spoken at the last supper:

> The kings of the Gentiles exercise lordship over them; and those in authority over them are called benefactors. But not

so with you; rather let the greatest among you become as the youngest, and the leader as one who serves. For which is the greater, one who sits at table, or one who serves? Is it not the one who sits at table? But I am among you as one who serves. (Lk 22:25–27)

And this is how that service unfolds:

And during supper, when the devil had already put it into the heart of Judas Iscariot, Simon's son, to betray him, Jesus, knowing that the Father had given all things into his hands, and that he had come from God and was going to God, rose from supper, laid aside his garments, and girded himself with a towel. Then he poured water into a basin, and began to wash the disciples' feet, and to wipe them with the towel with which he was girded. (Jn 13:2–5)

As Jesus rises from his reclining position at table, all eyes follow him. As he removes his outer garment, takes in hand a towel, pitcher and basin, attention turns to perplexity. Everyone can tell that the Master is intent on this cleaning ritual and does not want to be interrupted. Like a mother bathing her own children, he washes their feet carefully, deliberately, and with great gentleness. Each apostle asks himself, 'Why is he doing this?' And they are making eye contact with one another over Jesus' head as the Lord crawls from one man to the other. They shrug. They question one another with their eyes. But after all, it's not the first time they've seen the

Lord do something that they couldn't explain.

Once he took mud and made a blind man see. Another time he chose not to prevent his friend Lazarus from dying: and then he went and raised him from the tomb. And there were those times when thousands of people had followed Jesus into the wilderness and he refused to send them away when there was a shortage of food: and then he fed everyone. Everything eventually turned out okay. But this night everyone is confused. No miracle is forthcoming. It's different from anything they've ever seen before because it's so infinitely simple and servile. What's the point of this?

"Do you know what I have done to you?" is the Lord's question to his questioning men (Jn 13:12). It's as though the Lord is saying: *I have shown you something tonight that no one in the history of the world has ever seen before. I have done something for you that you have never experienced before. I have loved you. I have loved you in a way that no one has been loved before. I have given myself in a way that no one has ever given himself before.* When God bends the knee before his creatures, we see a display of humble service, of tender love, that should both (as Newman said earlier) *subdue* and *melt* us.

Is this what we need to see? When we see the Lord loving us by acting like a slave before us, is this really necessary? As hard as it is to watch Jesus at our feet, it is what we need to see to understand the love that he came to show us not only in the Eucharist, but in the Sacrament of Reconciliation. We need to see God washing the dirt off our feet. We need to see God *insisting* on washing the dirt off our feet. We need to hear God say that we cannot belong to him unless we let him do this for us.

God sinks to his hands and knees before us and takes responsibility for cleaning off the soil that we have put there, and in Jesus' eyes, *This means you belong to me. When you let me do this for you, you belong to me.* Do we understand this? The bridegroom whom I mentioned earlier told me prior to the wedding how he saw his call to marriage: "I just want to serve her." Isn't Jesus saying the same incredible, even embarrassing thing to us? The bride might look at herself and feel embarrassed by all the attention and care. She might feel unworthy. But she has to give in, because that's what it means to be a bride. You are loved and served first, and then the rest of your life is returning it, a lifelong surrender in love.

Take your most embarrassing moment, your most regrettable sin, the thing that you wish you could take back and can't, and imagine Jesus saying: *I make myself responsible for that. I'll answer for it. I'll take it on myself as though it were mine from start to finish.* We would say, *But, Lord, I can't let you do that. It's not fair. You shouldn't have to suffer for my failures.* And we know exactly what he will say: "If I do not wash you, you have no part in me" (Jn 13:8). Why? Because Jesus must love his own to the end. His love does not stop at our sins, but embraces us and our sins all together, and it is in the nearness of that embrace that we are both encouraged and compelled to part with all that impedes deeper closeness with him, to do the first thing

Jesus bids us do in his ministry: "Repent and believe in the gospel" (Mk 1:15).

Evoking the bridal imagery of the Old Testament, St. Bernard of Clairvaux makes the same point. God liberated Israel in the Exodus by first loving her in her captivity and then winning her heart by the gift of redemption.

> [God] was her lover even before she was freed from sin, for if he had not loved her he would not have set her free; it was through this gift of freedom that she was won over to become his love. St. John's words explain it: "It was not that we loved him, but first he loved us."[1]

Love needed to come first. Love was present well before the beloved bride was aware of being the object of saving love. But once recognition dawns on her, conversion is the only response that makes sense. When Jesus begins to operate like this in the New Testament by socializing with the moral outlaws and social outcasts of his day, he personally renews the ancient pattern of divine love. He does not mingle with "undesirables" because he can't get along with observant, respectable Jews, but because contact with Jesus is contact with God—and ready or not, in every generation God does the same thing, reaching out to those most in need of a Physician, but least likely to ask for one.

This is why people who practice their faith either unenthusiastically or not at all might find themselves inexplicably stirred—by a retreat, a sacred image, or a homily—to renounce degrading or undignified

1   Bernard of Clairvaux, *Sermons on the Song of Songs*, vol. 2 (Kalamazoo, Mich.: Cistercian Publications, 1971), p. 198.

ways, suddenly awakening like the prodigal son starving in the pigsty to the warmth and nourishment awaiting him in his father's house. God has touched them. And the pressure of that touch is enough to rock the boat of their prejudices about worldly happiness and fulfillment.

What has happened is conversion by contrast. God reveals some of his tender mercies, a ray of his purity and beauty to an individual, creating a dissonance with all the unworthy things that they had previously clung to—making them appear as worthless as they did to St. Paul: "Indeed I count everything as loss because of the surpassing worth of knowing Christ Jesus my Lord. For his sake I have suffered the loss of all things, and count them as refuse, in order that I may gain Christ and be found in him" (Phil 3:8–9).

God can and will use just about anything to get this all-important job done. After he empties himself and becomes a man, we can no longer cling to our preconceived ideas about what God should or should not do to reach us. This is precisely the scandal of the New Testament for those who objected to the Lord's *earthy* contact with the sick and sinners, with Gentiles; to many it seemed beneath God or any godly man to act in this way: mud to cure blindness, saliva applied to the tongue of the mute, a tax-paying fish with two coins in its gullet, curing leprosy by actually touching it, all the way to the Passion and the foot-washing that preceded it. God seems too intimately involved in human life, too close for comfort, that he takes material things too seriously—so seriously that he communicates grace through them.

That God acts this way in Christ Jesus will always be a sign of his incomprehensible humility, and a call to us for deeper and deeper humility. Many Christians outside the Church object to the fact that Catholics use things such as beads, water, oil, bread, and wine to come into contact with God. And to be honest, there will always be marginal Catholics who are embarrassed to use these things because of the humility required for their use.

But God started it. No one can blame Catholics for using holy oil, for example, since the apostles themselves used it on mission, and someone with greater authority—one greater than the temple and greater than Solomon—must have told them to do so (See: Mk 6:12–13). Likewise for the command to wash one another's feet as a symbol for forgiving sins, and the giving of the Spirit in the upper room as the power to forgive and retain sins (See: Jn 20:22–23). Fidelity to the Master requires that we take these instructions seriously.

Like most people, I suppose, I seldom think about this scene in the upper room when I go to confession. I think more about my own need for pardon and peace. I think about how good it is to feel forgiven and free and to start over again. I am often amazed at how simple the whole process of reconciliation is, speaking here both as priest and penitent. And although on the night he was betrayed the Giver of the Eucharist and of Reconciliation groaned in anguish over his betrayal, sweat blood, was troubled that his best friends were incapable of staying awake and praying with Him, and had trembling hands and a wounded heart—all he wants to do is to serve us. It means everything to him.

To see confession as Jesus serving is not an innovation, but gospel.

The Master of the household has always doubled as a steward: "Blessed are those servants whom the master finds awake when he comes; truly, I say to you, he will gird himself and have them sit at table, and he will come and serve them" (Lk 12:37).

The Son of Man came not to be served, but to serve, and to serve by ransoming. Ransom buys back captives, hostages, the kidnapped, and this declares our status without Christ: chained up, in bondage. We are in need of a redemption payable by God alone, with the coinage we all can identify. No waving of a magic wand will do, but a body prepared for God to serve and suffer in, to love through. This is what we need to be served by (See: Heb 10:5).

Jesus' service has nothing to do with the common forms of hired service we all know, such as at restaurants and hotels. By his own testimony the Lord is not a "hireling" (See: Jn 10:12). The Lord serves by emptying himself and laying down his life, so that everything he does for us is pure and *infinite* self-gift, underwritten by his flesh and blood, backed by the total evacuation of himself in the Incarnation. Jesus,

> though he was in the form of God, did not count equality with God a thing to be grasped, but emptied himself, taking the form of a servant, being born in the likeness of men. And being found in human form he humbled himself and became obedient unto death, even death on a cross. (Phil 2:5–8)

You can't get lower, more servile, or more loving than that. And Jesus didn't do it for any reason other than making the incomprehensible love of God a little less incomprehensible. Maybe we don't pay close enough attention to God's love in our lives, his stooping down to us without shaming or condescension, somewhat as we take for granted the domestic service of family life. But maybe when God shows up at our feet prepared to do something that we ourselves might shrink from doing for another, then we will get the message. Jesus wants to cleanse us, so that we will be clean in the most important ways: washed clean of lies, double-dealing, selfishness, self-indulgence and severity, anything that requires a shadowy cover to carry out. But most of all, the Lord cleanses us by restoring dignity, making coexistence with unworthy ways no longer tolerable for us. "Purge me with hyssop, and I shall be clean," begs the psalmist, "wash me, and I shall be whiter than snow" (Ps 51:7).

Although sin normally disguises itself as freedom or self-actualization, it always ends up diminishing self-worth and leaves us open to the very real danger of despair. The devil especially exploits, often successfully, the human tendency to forfeit the fight and say, *I'm too far gone now. No use trying to climb a mountain I know I'm going to slide down again.* And so people avoid confession because of the insurmountable look of their moral landscape.

But that is all a lie, a deception aimed at keeping us down, depressed, and discouraged. If that creepy episode in the Gospel of a "legion" of devils petitioning Jesus to be let loose into a herd of swine teaches us anything (See: Mk 5:1–20), it shows us what Satan's final goal is for all of us: self-destruction, death, damnation. Those swine immediately rushed into the sea and all were drowned. What the devils were not allowed to do to the man whom they had been tormenting, they did to mere animals. And Jesus wants us to witness that along with the bystanders in Gerasa and be terrified at the brutal malice of the evil one.

Against that very avoidable fate, Jesus comes before us with water, basin, and towel, just wanting to serve us by the cleansing of confession. In confession and reconciliation, we will find new strength, new dignity, new love each time we let the Lord wash us clean.

And against the ugliness of evil, sin, and death comes the promise of nuptial intimacy that Jesus wants with each of us. Just as Christian husbands and wives love each other in holy matrimony, so does Jesus take us to himself to purify our uncleanness that we may be joined to him always, without doubt or shame, but with wholehearted surrender to his love.

> Husbands, love your wives, as Christ loved the church and gave himself up for her, that he might sanctify her, having cleansed her by the washing of water with the word, that he might present the church to himself in splendor, without spot or wrinkle or any such thing, that she might be holy and without blemish. Even so husbands should love their wives as their own bodies. He who loves his wife loves himself. For no man ever hates his own flesh, but nourishes and cherishes it, as Christ does the church, because we are members of his body. (Eph 5:25–30)

CHAPTER SEVEN
Homecoming for the Children of God: Mary, Our Refuge

The children of men take refuge in the shadow of thy wings. Oh to be safe under the shelter of thy wings!

–PSALMS 36:7; 61:4

A priest who had been a chaplain in Vietnam during the war once told me the story of what happened to him when he had been captured. Having been stripped of his clothing, he was tied to a stake outdoors, exposed to the elements. And it began to rain, the pounding rain of a tropical climate, often broken by moments of intense sunlight and heat, before starting up again. It was a type of the dark night of the soul spoken of by the great masters of spirituality, but now fleshed out in one man's solitary life, in a singularly brutal solitude.

At a certain point he saw God out of the corner of his eye: A mother hen was protecting her chicks under outstretched wings as the rain relentlessly fell. It was then, he said, that he understood the Lord's use of that image in the Gospel more deeply than ever before: "How often would I have gathered your children together as a hen gathers her brood under her wings" (Lk 13:34). In this case, experience was everything. He knew the verse, the simile, but never before had he known as deeply the Lord's compassion, as well as his own radical need for divine overshadowing. The experience of total vulnerability brought home the intensity of the Lord's love: "For thou hast been my help, and in the shadow of thy wings I sing for joy. My soul clings to thee; thy right hand upholds me" (Ps 63:7-8).

Reflected in this story is not only how God loves us, but how we grow to perceive his love. The kiss, the embrace, so integral to human love, must surrender its natural comfort before the standard of divine love, which kisses and embraces with an intimacy that, we might say, disconcerts and even terrifies.[1] Those, for example, who stood by and watched while a deceased youth borne en route to his grave was commanded by Jesus to live again, were "seized with fear" when the young man sat up in his coffin (See: Lk 7:11–16). Sorrow suddenly inverted into rapture generates a terror edged with ecstasy that can only be called divine. For more on this, pay close attention whenever Jesus boards a boat in the Gospels!

1   More on the divine "kiss" and "embrace" could not come from a more credible witness than St. Teresa of Calcutta: "Look at the cross and you will see Jesus' head bent to kiss you, his arms extended to embrace you, his heart opened to receive you, to enclose you with his love." As quoted in Edward Le Joly, *Mother Teresa of Calcutta: A Biography* (San Francisco: Harper & Row, 1983), p. 333.

What is standard in God's love needs learning. That the chaplain was in a place of great dereliction and *continued* to suffer as the Lord revealed that little scene to him is very instructive. Although he continued to agonize, now he could interpret his suffering in a new light. The Lord had neither abandoned nor forgotten him. God was raising him to a higher level of trust, abandonment, and love. What an intimate exchange it is between the Lord and us when we are in a tight spot, when we feel forsaken, and the Lord drops a little reminder that he's got everything accounted for. *You think I've forgotten you? You think that your prayer life is all a dream? You think that the Gospels are legends? You think I don't mean it when I say that all of the hairs of your head are numbered? Heaven and earth will pass away, but my words will never pass away.*

With gospel simplicity, Christians have always felt very comfortable gathering themselves around the Mother of Jesus as a brood of chicks beneath sheltering wings. "Comfortable" is probably not a strong enough word; *compelled* is more like it. In fact, the most ancient prayer to Mary, apart from the Gospel-inspired "Hail Mary," is a prayer of escape: the *Sub tuum praesidium* ("Under Your Protection"). Originating as early as the third century, its requests are simple and heartfelt:

We fly to thy protection,
O holy Mother of God.
Despise not our petitions
in our necessities,
but deliver us always

from all dangers

O glorious and blessed Virgin.[2]

From New Testament times forward, Christians have made no bones about needing a spiritual refuge. Our Lord, from the cross, paved the way to it by mutually entrusting his mother and St. John to each other (See: Jn 19:26–27). This is more than a detail revealing filial conscientiousness on the part of Jesus. After all, he was to rise again in three days, at which point he could have made further provision for her. No, John notes this entrustment because its scope exceeds a relationship of caretaking between two individuals. It is all disciples of all times who inherit the motherhood of Mary; all those "who keep the commandments of God and bear testimony to Jesus" are counted her children by the Scriptures (Rev 12:17).

A refuge is for running to, whether it's protection from the weather or from enemy fire. You run to it unashamed at your need for shelter, ready to rejoice with others who have found their way in. You are not at all embarrassed at associating with fellow refugees who may be tattered and worn-out, like the survivors of a deluge. The same desperate need brings all together under the same mantle. It is enough that everyone made it, that they found safety when they could have been lost.

Before going any further, it should be said that this chapter is aimed both at those hesitating to fly to Mary's protection and those

2   *Compendium of the Catechism of the Catholic Church*, Appendix A: Common Prayers (Washington, D.C.: USCCB, 2009), p. 184. http://www.vatican.va/archive/compendium_ccc/documents/archive_2005_compendium-ccc_en.html.

who do it only sporadically. The message here is simple: We must live under her protection always, as St. John is said to have taken Mary into his home or "to his own," as the Douay version has it. The idea conveys far more than *housing* the Mother of God; it means taking her into one's life, living with and under her as Jesus did.

Let's be honest about our own attempts at self-protection, most especially against sin and temptation. Our own defenses do not get the job done. We say yes when we should say no, and no when we should say yes. A shelter stronger than our own will is required, which for any of us can be pretty flimsy when iron is what we need. We need a beauty in our lives that is strong and constant as iron, yet with a delicacy that gentles us. Tenderness toward God through his holy Mother is what Jesus teaches us from the cross (not to mention through his infancy), and it is this tenderness that wears away the toughness produced by repeated sin. As the hardness softens, as the ice melts, conversion follows apace.

The regrettable but understandable reflex of sinners is to keep their distance from what is pure and holy. And this has some merit: God certainly does not want us to get so casual with holy people and things that we put the sacred and profane on equal footing. In churches, there is such a place as a sanctuary for a reason. Sacred vestments and vessels are used in celebrating the Eucharist for a reason. And most importantly, our souls need to be right with God before approaching Holy Communion—for an especially important reason. "Holy things to the holy" cries the priest prior to holy communion in many Eastern liturgies, serving as much to affirm the goodness and dignity of the communicant as to remind all of the need for self-examination.

But a warped view of holiness caricatures the sanctity of the Blessed Virgin and the saints into something less than human—unreal, unapproachable, and unsympathetic. By all means, remove your sandals when on holy ground. But remember that the first one who did that had killed a man out of anger and then hid his crime. Then he fled the authorities. But in his hiding place in the land of Midian, God caught his eye from afar in a fiery bush, and introduced himself as an old family friend (See: Ex 2–3). Reverence and healthy familiarity go together.

Being a flesh-and-blood human among the pristine beauty of marble statuary might inspire shame at having a pulse, digestive track, respiratory system, etc., whatever makes us aware of being bodily creatures. But it distorts human holiness. "I have never liked biographies of saints," complains St. Josemaria,

> which naively—but also with a lack of sound doctrine—present their deeds as if they had been confirmed in grace from birth. No. The true life stories of Christian heroes resemble our own experience: they fought and won; they fought and lost. And then, repentant, they returned to the fray.[3]

If we feel like we don't belong among such rarified beings as martyrs, confessors, virgins, and most especially the Mother

3 Escrivá, *Christ is Passing By*, no. 76.

of God, it might be because we think they're made of something other than human stuff. If we judge our sins as *too* embarrassing or irremediable, we will think it pure hypocrisy to drop to our knees before their images to ask for help, as though they were made of the same material as their images!

The idea of former sins and ongoing temptations making one a hypocrite is common enough. Or the fact that one is still dazzled and allured by shameful things makes people balk at presenting themselves before the Immaculate Conception, who seems likely to turn away in disgust. But if we don't understand what kind of glue bonds the communion of saints, then *keep-away* is the only game we'll play—as in some countries (or cultures) where the women and children attend Sunday Mass on the inside of the church while the men loiter, often smoking, on the porch outside.

If past delinquency and present frailty are considered too off-putting for the Mother of God, let it be known that one such as St. Augustine felt the same way: an irresistible draw to holiness versus an oppressive revulsion at his own perversity. This is how he resolved it, or how it was resolved for him, in the moment of his conversion. Tormented by past sins against chastity and distressed by the pull they continued to exert over him, he describes a moral drama in which he is "overcome with shame" and "hanging in suspense." This long excerpt forms the centerpiece of his crisis, the conclusion of his conflict, and it has rescued many from the straits of sheer despair.

I was held back by all my old attachments. They plucked at

the garment of my flesh and whispered, "Are you going to dismiss us? From this moment we shall never be with you again, for ever and ever. From this moment you will never again be allowed to do this thing or that, for evermore." In my state of indecision, [these voices] kept me from tearing myself away, from shaking myself free of them and leaping across the barrier to the other side, where you were calling me. Habit was too strong for me when it asked, "Do you think you can live without these things?"

But I had turned my eyes elsewhere, and while I stood trembling at the barrier, on the other side I could see the chaste beauty of Continence in all her serene, unsullied joy, as she modestly beckoned me to cross over and to hesitate no more. She stretched out loving hands to welcome and embrace me. She was not barren but a fruitful mother of children, of joys born of you, O Lord, her Spouse. She smiled at me to give me courage, as though she were saying, "Can you not do what these men and women do? Do you think they find the strength to do it in themselves and not in the Lord their God? Cast yourself upon God and have no fear, for he will welcome you and cure you of your ills." [4]

Reading Augustine's transparent account, we can't help but see the personified Continence or Chastity as a mirror image of the Blessed

4 Augustine, *Confessions*, 8.11, pp. 175–176. Selection abridged by author.

Virgin *beckoning*, stretching out loving hands to welcome and embrace. She is surrounded not by the strong, not by the undefeated, but by those who have learned to cling to the Lord in confidence while entrusting themselves to her motherly care. And her very pointed question "Do you think they're doing this all by themselves?" takes the wind out of our objections, exposes the dubious humility that uses its guiltiness as a shield to deflect the encouraging smile of this fruitful mother.

That the Blessed Mother stands as a rallying point for spiritual refugees means that she unites the children of God especially under the traditional title of "Refuge of Sinners." Although sin is what often divides people not only from God but from one another, and indeed creates inner division as well, love is unitive. And our Lady radiates a love that draws all to herself whose hearts are open to partake of a common mercy, even with our other differences intact.

St. Josemaría describes congregating around her as a kind of family reunion:

> Seeing how so many Christians express their affection for the Virgin Mary, surely you also feel more a part of the Church, closer to those brothers and sisters of yours. It is like a family reunion. Grown-up children, whom life has separated, come back to their mother for some family anniversary. And even if they have not always got on well together, today things are different; they feel united, sharing the same affection.[5]

---

5   Escrivá, *Christ is Passing By*, no. 139.

Overcoming division of any kind requires the wisdom to focus first on what unites. St. Paul, after recounting the misdeeds of his pre-conversion days, says that he was "treated mercifully" as an example for the rest of us (See: 1 Tm 1:12–17). If merciful treatment is the model for God's dealings with us, then the most meaningful bond we have with one another is the shared gift of God's merciful love. The New Testament unfolds the effects of this love in declaring a oneness among believers transcending distinctions of male and female, race, and social status. These are the distinctly far-reaching effects of baptism, whose power gathers into one all whom sin had previously driven far apart.

The Scriptures challenge us with this language of unity and mercy. The Gospel would have us put all people (the just and unjust, friend and enemy) on equal footing. Jesus would have us forgive as he forgives, to love even those who mistreat us. Whether they are sorry or not is beside the point. We are not asked to approve or condone anything evil, nor to forgo the pursuit of justice, but to refrain from judging what only God can see and evaluate with true equity.

Having a sense of our common need for mercy opens the way to deeper kinship, one capable of outlasting both petty and serious offenses, finally carrying over into an everlasting union in the glory of heaven. Whenever we honor Mary not only as Mother but as our *refuge* we acknowledge this enduring union as already begun. "Enduring" because as our refuge Mary is Mother of Mercy, and the chief occupation of the blessed in heaven is to surround the throne of God with hymns of praise and thanksgiving, most especially for the mercies by which we are saved: "I will sing of thy steadfast love, O Lord, for ever" (Ps 89:1).

Although the idea of "refuge" suggests safe haven from dangers to which one's forces are unequal, our Lady's role is more than, say, a demilitarized zone. In her we find not merely a neutral space, but the harbor, the sanctuary, where all life's hurts are understood by one whose life was overshadowed by a prophecy of piercing sorrow and punctuated by its full enactment. This explains why Mary's motherhood over us is best displayed by how it flourishes under the cross of her Son. Her heart is more open beneath the cross than at any other moment in her earthly life.

As Mother of the Redeemer she does not abandon her Son, but carries out her unique motherhood to the very end by a heartfelt sharing in everything Jesus suffers. As mothers regularly absorb the sufferings of their children, so does the Blessed Mother spiritually take on those of her Son. Nor does she ever abandon *God's scattered children*, who are the fruit of those sufferings (See: Jn 11:52).

"The Divine Redeemer," says St. John Paul II, wishes to penetrate the soul of every sufferer through the heart of his holy Mother, the first and the most exalted of all the redeemed. As though by a continuation of that motherhood which by the power of the Holy Spirit had given him life, the dying Christ conferred upon the ever Virgin Mary a *new kind of motherhood*—spiritual and universal—towards all human beings, so that every individual, during the pilgrimage of faith, might remain, together with her, closely united to him unto the Cross, and so that every form of suffering, given fresh life by the power of this Cross, should become no longer the weakness of man but the power of God.[6]

Looking into her suffering heart, we find a love wholly unique opening out to us. At the same time her heart is virginal, maternal, and impeccable. A love woven of these three strands—purity, maternity, sinlessness—reveals a heart of the greatest breadth and therefore of unparalleled suffering. Yet the heart of the sorrowful Virgin is not narrowed by suffering, as ours are apt to shrink and withdraw in painful moments. Our Lady's heart expands in her affliction to embrace in spirit all that Jesus embraces on the cross— not only his sufferings, but also those for whom he suffers.

"In Mary's case," St. John Paul II says beautifully, "we have a special and exceptional mediation."[7]

Mary became not only the "nursing mother" of the Son of Man but also the "associate of unique nobility" of the Messiah and Redeemer. ...[S]he advanced in her pilgrimage of faith, and in this pilgrimage to the foot of the Cross there was simultaneously accomplished her maternal cooperation

6   John Paul II, Apostolic Letter on the Christian Meaning of Human Suffering *Salvifici doloris* (February 11, 1984), 26.

7   John Paul II, Encyclical Letter on the Blessed Virgin Mary in the Life of the Pilgrim Church *Redemptoris Mater* (March 25, 1987), 39. http://w2.vatican.va/content/john-paul-ii/en/encyclicals/documents/hf_jp-ii_enc_25031987_redemptoris-mater.html.

with the Savior's whole mission through her actions and sufferings. Along the path of this collaboration with the work of her Son, the Redeemer, Mary's motherhood itself underwent a singular transformation, becoming ever more imbued with "burning charity" towards all those to whom Christ's mission was directed. Through this "burning charity," which sought to achieve, in union with Christ, the restoration of "supernatural life to souls," Mary entered, in a way all her own, into the one mediation "between God and men" which is the mediation of the man Christ Jesus.[8]

From ancient times, Christian piety has always led the faithful to enter into, gather under, the mantle of her unique mediation. Nothing could be more natural for the children of God. Her sorrows, in a special way, attract her children. The sight of Mary at the foot of the cross, veiled and garbed in somber robes, speaks to the faithful yet suffering soul. As Jesus' human life was slowly extinguished, she remained the one light shining, the one inextinguishable lamp burning in the darkest of places, although her suffering did not diminish.

At the moment of our Lord's arrest he had said to those apprehending him: "But this is your hour, and the power of darkness" (Lk 22:53). That same darkness falls from time to time on the disciples of Jesus, upon us. This is why Mary must be our refuge: She knows what it is to remain constant when darkness falls upon the Christian soul. And it does fall, because to live for Jesus in this

8   *Redemptoris Mater.*

world means that we will come into open conflict with evil—within ourselves first, and then in the world around us. There are times when we too feel the pain of misunderstandings, of unfair treatment, of confusion. And Jesus gives us his Mother so that we will look to her, as he did, in those moments. We can imagine her encouraging us with these words from Job:

> Surely then you will lift up your face without blemish; you will be secure, and will not fear. You will forget your misery; you will remember it as waters that have passed away. And your life will be brighter than the noonday; its darkness will be like the morning. And you will have confidence, because there is hope. (Job 11:15–18)

Such encouragement can only come from the heart of one who has passed through the darkness of discipleship with an unwavering confidence in the Lord. Indeed, we can only imagine all of the appalling sights and sounds that surrounded her as she remained near the cross. Exposed to more than the natural environment, she contended with the far worse human elements: the reviling, the brutality, etc. And amid all of the noise and commotion, our Lady also had to listen to the commentary of her Son's enemies:

> And those who passed by derided him, wagging their heads and saying, "You who would destroy the temple and build it in three days, save yourself! If you are the Son of God, come down from the cross." ... "He saved others; he cannot save

himself. He is the King of Israel; let him come down now from the cross, and we will believe in him. He trusts in God; let God deliver him now, if he desires him; for he said, 'I am the Son of God.'" And the robbers who were crucified with him also reviled him in the same way. (See: Mt 27:39–43)

This unruly and brutal environment was the setting in which our Lady's maternal vocation reached its crowning moment.

Now the point of this side trip to Calvary is to make graphic the reality of a woman with true tears, a heart really stabbed with pain, and thus lay down the full weight of Mary's role as refuge. Just as she could pity all of the confused, callous, and ignorant characters who came and went around her Son's cross, so can she look with compassion on us all, even when we're acting in confused, callous, and foolish ways. Those whom we find hardest to get along with, whom we struggle to love, whom we might judge too hastily and unfairly—they, along with us, are welcome to this homecoming or family reunion because they too have need of refuge, of mercy. At least one among the detachment of soldiers on Calvary, we call him St. Longinus, responded to the grace of the event, as our Lady looked on, rapt in pain and prayer. "Truly this was the Son of God!" was his confession (Mt 27:54).

Everyone enters this world as an outcast. Having been cast out of paradise, out of a banquet, much of what we do—both good and bad—is a form of "gate crashing," trying to reestablish ourselves in a condition of happiness and peace. We all intuit, or at least feel restless enough to suspect, that we were born to live in this place—yet at the same time a feeling of unworthiness clings to every aspiration for it. All of this amounts to appreciating mercy as a shared gift among the children of God, as the cement that bonds us. It is what makes us children of God in the first place.

Those motley characters invited to the marriage banquet in the Lord's parable (the "B" list) were virtually dragged in off the streets, but at least they came, accepting what the King was offering at no cost (Mt 22:1–14). They came from different walks of life, perhaps with dissimilar interests and abilities, but all stood in need of what the banquet hall could offer. The Host and his table were appreciated by those who saw they had no right to be there, but *needed to be.*

Unlike the followers and fans of the virtual world, this fellowship is a true one, not a pretend communion of persons, and we call it the "communion of saints." It is not an elite club of the already perfect, but the bond in Christ of all who belong to him at all stages of Christian development. Baptized infants, catechumens, those fallen into sin, those consecrated to God's service, the struggling, the victorious—all have their place in Christ.

The Lord offers many images of what his kingdom looks like and almost invariably it is a flock of latecomers, rescued wanderers, "sinners and tax collectors" ready to leave their old life for the new. Jesus came not to save angels but human sinners. No matter how committed or devout a disciple is, he will still fall periodically. No one can safely omit "And lead us not into temptation, but deliver us from evil" from their prayers. No one, not even a saint, can consider confession superfluous.

Establishing the fact of our shared sinfulness, however, does not tell the whole story about what unites us. It remains a negative, like those whose kinship is formed from a shared disease or disability. But as with the handicaps that unite so many, a positive can emerge from a fellowship of disadvantages that creates a sense of welcome, comradery, acceptance, even of strength. Often the first and biggest step is having the willingness to approach and join up with others, which is admittedly made more difficult if the umbrella you stand under features a "minus" sign, broadcasting your weakness, your deficits, your less-than status.

The cross is that sign for us. It has been seen as a mark of shame, a stumbling block, an absurdity, since day one. The ultimate sign of weakness, defeat, and helplessness will always be a scandal to some. It will always demand humility of those who stand in its shade. And it will always stand as the uncontested, sole means of victory over sin and death, for those willing to do more than just think about it. This is another case where experience is everything. Until you scrape the depths of your own poverty, you will never know the power of the Lord's cross to deliver you: "For he was crucified in weakness, but lives by the power of God. For we are weak in him, but ... we shall live with him by the power of God" (2 Cor 13:4).

One of the most admirable secular instances of the public avowal of personal weakness is the willingness of individuals to attend Twelve-Step meetings to declare their dependence on substances and their desire to be free from addiction. Even more impressive are those who line up outside of a confessional in an ordinary parish church to declare their sinfulness, unconcerned about what anyone else might think. But behind the willingness to do either is the memory of a mother's arms; the child's natural instinct to retreat to mom when in danger, frightened, or failed translates into adult moral life by a humble readiness to admit one's need.

The hen and her chicks, beneath a torrent or under the blistering sun, is (like the sign of Jonah) a revelation of God's weakness outstripping human power, outwitting the wisdom of this world, conquering while giving every appearance of frailty.

It is fitting that Jesus would keynote his public ministry in this way, inaugurating it in a setting, a wedding feast, where he supplies for a potentially public and embarrassing human failure. And more, the Blessed Virgin is instrumental in drawing this mercy from her Son on our behalf. "The mother of Jesus said to him," making our cause her own, "'They have no wine'" (See: Jn 2:1–10). These facts have never been lost on Christians.

Jesus wants us to see our entire earthly journey as a path to getting back inside where we all belong: at table in the wedding banquet, in the mansion with many rooms—no longer in a temporary refuge but home forever in the Father's house.

CHAPTER EIGHT

The Love of His Heart
and the Work of His Hands:
Saint Joseph

[St. Joseph] is someone who unites inner recollection and promptness. From the open tent of his life he is inviting us to withdraw a little from the tumult of the senses; to recover our inner recollection; to learn to look inside ourselves and to look up, so that God can touch our souls and speak his word to us.

–JOSEPH RATZINGER (POPE BENEDICT XVI)[1]

Pretty much the first things to jump off the pages of the New Testament are the paradoxes of the Gospel: that life is found in dying like a grain of wheat, that the loss of everything for Christ leads to the gain of all things in him, that greatness comes from littleness and service. These and other

---

1   Homily given by Joseph Ratzinger, Rome (March 19, 1992). https://gloria.tv/article/4shswB3Zqgda1XJpH8DGSfmx3.

seeming contradictions challenge and perplex us, just as they did our Lord's first listeners. But perplexity and challenge have a way of making inroads to our minds and hearts, and the Lord most surely knows this. He wants us to process apparent incompatibles to arrive at the truth about life, love, and salvation.

The same kind of processing is necessary for other gospel contraries that will always be irreconcilable: that good fruit cannot issue from bad trees; that both God and riches (or mammon) cannot be served equally; that, as St. Paul says, one cannot partake of the Eucharist while engaging in idolatry, which amounts to the same thing as serving God and mammon. There is a boundary between light and darkness that cannot be straddled without placing oneself in a state of spiritual infidelity or adultery, as the scriptures consider idolatry to be.

A further paradox suggests itself, though perhaps not crystalized into a saying of the Lord: *You cannot serve God on the condition that you understand, much less approve of, even less are consulted about, everything he will ask of you ahead of time.* If following another obviously requires knowledge of a path or visible footprints, then the paradox is plain. But following the God of Israel, following Jesus Christ, involves more than knowing how many miles till the next turn. Our Lord's memorable rejoinder to Thomas the Apostle's complaint, "Lord, we do not know where you are going; how can we know the way?" is the golden rule of discipleship: "I am the way, and the truth, and the life; no one comes to the Father, but by me" (Jn 14:5–6).

The New Testament opens with this golden rule, not so much in words as in the deeds of St. Joseph, the Lord's foster-father.

Although Scripture discloses precious little about St. Joseph, words such as 'faithful,' 'just,' 'obedient,' and 'silent' always seem apt to describe his character. And although his mouth never opens in any recorded statement, his ears and heart are always open wide, listening to God, as Pope Benedict says above. We know this by how he responds: immediately, trustingly. St. Joseph is a faithful follower, and because he is, his leadership is second to none. He guides his beloved Mary and her divine Child in and out of Palestine, across foreign borders, making do with whatever God provides.

The Gospels make known his trade: He was a craftsman. And this fact combined with what we know about his heart, that he loved Jesus and Mary more than anything, makes us ask: Are there more important "facts" to know about a man? Isn't this more than enough to go on? You can tell a man's character by the love of his life and the work of his hands. The woman he chooses to love, to marry, and to stay with for life, and the quality of his work, however humble and hidden it might be—that is what makes a man a man.

What makes a man not only good but a saint, however, is how he responds to God. Nature drives a man to work and to marry. Grace moves him to make of marriage and work an offering acceptable to God. And it is here that St. Joseph's odyssey of obedience to God's will unfolds.

Our Lady and St. Joseph, in the days surrounding our Lord's birth, surrender to what God asks, what he gives, and what he takes. They leave Nazareth, go to Bethlehem, and stay in Egypt. There is not much stability and not much assurance about what tomorrow will bring. They arrive in Bethlehem and cannot stay in comfortable quarters. They go to the stable, and soon after Jesus is born must pick up and move again, into the house where the Magi will find the holy child. Then it's a midnight flight as refugees to Egypt for an unspecified length of time, until they can return and finally live in Nazareth, Judea being too dangerous. If John the Baptist was prophesied to prepare the way of the Lord by making straight his paths, these paths were still very crooked when the Lord entered our world. Inconveniences and harrowing escapes are the order of the day.

Our closeness to God shows itself when we can embrace difficulties with peace and detachment, just as St. Joseph and Mary did without any apparent complaint—not without hardship, but without protest. Their attitude was: *If the only place for Jesus' birth is a stable, then we will make the stable work. That will be our home for as long as God wills. If it is to Egypt that we must go and stay for an indefinite time, then we will make it work. It will be our home for as long as God wills.* And why? Because they both knew and trusted the Father, not a roadmap or timetable; trust in God was their guide. In St. Joseph we honor a man who was not only good, humble, and a hardworking provider for his family, but one who lovingly and prayerfully made God's choices his own.

All of this is real. The stories are true; the individuals involved are real people; the dangers are real; the ruthlessness of personages such as Herod is not exaggerated. This is a way of saying that uniting yourself to God's will as Joseph did is not as easy as checking a box or clicking a link. He had to do what many men find hardest to do: listen to God with an open heart and a docile will.

Men are typically problem-solvers and results-oriented, even in matters of faith. Waiting on the Lord, being uncertain about the next move, and feeling passive are not easy postures for men to settle into. Abraham, Job, Jonah, and many others either chafed against waiting or were vexed by apparent misdirection. Yet they went the distance. And this is the only way for a truly righteous man to live before God. The "manliest" of men are not those who intimidate, who don't take no for an answer. They are, in the words of St. James, "doers of the word, and not hearers only" (Jas 1:22). The courage that we associate with great and strong men is never more admirable than when a man of God takes God at his word and walks and works by faith.

A case in point is the gospel story of the Finding in the Temple (Lk 1:41–52), often read on the liturgical Solemnity of St. Joseph. It just might break all the rules for discipleship. Jesus asks to be followed, but here he has effectively hidden himself from his parents, staying behind in Jerusalem without notifying anyone. He knows that Mary and Joseph will return in search of him, experiencing an anxiety that Mary herself describes as "great." But he chooses to allow their distress in order to bear witness, even as a boy, to the supremacy of the Father's will, which he will later call not only his *work* but also his *food*.

It's easy for us to look back and see the whole story, to proclaim it as gospel from the pulpit, but it wasn't an easy history for Mary and

Joseph to be a part of. We have the whole episode neatly compacted into a Lectionary selection and a decade of the Rosary, and we can contemplate the mystery without any anxiety. The story has a beginning, a middle, and an end. But the holy couple had to live it firsthand, without script or stage directions to consult, without foreknowledge of the outcome. They were compelled to find the Lord not by prophetic insight but by process of elimination. One place after another proved fruitless until they decided to go up to the Lord's house.

Our lives unfold like that, without a ready-made timeline of events for reference. If we could see the end at the beginning, and all the steps in between, although we might be shocked at where God takes us, still we might still have greater peace in knowing where both our journeys and layovers are taking us. God does not want that for us. He wants us to follow in trust—and not just any kind of trust, but something on par with that of Mary and Joseph.

We needn't hesitate to call it a *blind* trust, because to human eyes faith will always be an obscurity, even as it is the lamp that lights our way. We follow not because all of the details, the detours, have been reviewed and "okayed" by us beforehand, not because we see the marvelous panoramic harmony of providence, but because God is the trailblazer of our path. Confidence in his wisdom and goodness, above all his love, decides how far our trust will go and thus how far we will follow.

Still, knowing all of this by faith and living it out in practice doesn't exempt us from the same kind of anxiety and incomprehension that troubled the hearts of Mary and Joseph in the wake of the unprecedented disappearance: "Son, why have you treated us so? Behold, your father and I have been looking for you anxiously" (Lk 2:48). Although Mary and Joseph never stopped trusting God, the emotional pain of loss stung. And certainly, as St. Josemaria observes, "Souls who know what it is to lose Jesus Christ and to find him again, are able to understand this."[2]

Mary and Joseph do not fully understand Jesus' response to Mary's very direct question: "Son, why have you treated us so?" What a question to ask of Jesus! What a complaint to make to God! Is this even acceptable? The endless conflict between God's ways and human ways shows itself even in our Lady and St. Joseph. They too had to look God in the face and ask "Why?"

We can all relate. When God acts in ways that completely surprise us, when he allows a lot of anxiety that we think could have been avoided, we might be tempted to think: Had we been informed ahead of time, had there been some consultation or "better planning" involved, then we could have responded without loss of time or composure.

But when God's ways are not at all what we had expected, we are forced to confront ourselves with a question: *I believe* in God, *but do I really believe* him? *Do I trust* him? Trust is the foundation of every good relationship. If we don't trust, we can't share ourselves with another, because we don't want to risk the insecurity that vulnerability

2   Escrivá, *Friends of God*, no. 53.

entails. We like to have insurance, money in the bank, a safety net, so that we can both practice our religion and otherwise get by with peace of mind. It's not wrong to have money or insurance. But it is wrong to serve God with a contingency plan to fall back on if his providence proves too unwieldy. St. Josemaria would call this "the risky security of the Christian."[3]

In the gospel of The Finding in the Temple, Jesus puts his divine finger on a place that only he can touch—the place of our anxieties and fears—and he says, *But I was always here. Do not be afraid.* And in uniquely divine fashion he consoles while challenging, alarms while reassuring. Standing in the temple with the holy couple, we can see where the loss and finding was leading. Jesus was always safe. He chose to be where he was. And in order for me to join him where he is, which is Jesus' explicit wish (See: Jn 14:3), doesn't my path need to follow something like the one traced out by Mary and Joseph? Can I reach God, can I mature as a human being, if I am not challenged to find and serve God? How can I tell what I truly want unless I am made to search? It is often in the searching that our true motives and priorities are revealed. Unless we have to stick to something, we can never tell how committed we are. Or if everything makes sense to me, if no surprises or contradictions ever cross my path, how can I tell if my path is the narrow and strict or wide and easy one?

When the story of St. Joseph in some way replays itself in *my life*, the mystery starts all over again. When God's choices *for me* are

3   Escrivá, *Christ is Passing By*, no. 58.

perplexing, the incomprehension begins anew. And we see more and more why Mary and Joseph are the models for how to respond to God without having all of our questions answered.

They are companions in surrender to God's will. The Church condenses the greatness of St. Joseph into practically one title: *Spouse of the Mother of God*. If St. Joseph is our Lady's fitting companion, her match, then more than being good friends or simply being "compatible," they are one in God, seeking the one thing necessary together—at whatever cost.

Whether their surrender takes them to a Bethlehem stable, to Egypt for an undetermined length of time, or on a three-day search for their lost child, they are prepared to do anything, go anywhere, as soon as the Lord makes his will known—even when he conveys it quietly by withdrawing from them in the temple. But it is there, in his Father's house, in a moment of great trial and incomprehension, that Jesus unravels the mystery with a mystery: God's will, being about the Father's business, is the ultimate goal of all faithful surrender, finally reached by way of trust.

Saints are not panicky people. When things go wrong, they trust. They may struggle, they may suffer, but they trust. St. Joseph certainly felt many anxieties, but he never doubted that the God who commands will also provide a way. As soon as he found out that God would be born of the Holy Virgin, to whom he was happily betrothed, the tone was set for the rest of their married life. No path would ever be too long, rough, or foreign, not even a nocturnal escape to Egypt.

In a way, the tone has also been set for our own life journey, set by St. Joseph's trust and courage. As disciples of Christ, our walk of faith may not allow us to see beyond the next step. But for the friend of God and companion of Mary, it will always be just enough.

CHAPTER NINE
A Better Homeland

For people who speak thus make it clear that they are seeking a homeland. If they had been thinking of that land from which they had gone out, they would have had opportunity to return. But as it is, they desire a better country, that is, a heavenly one. Therefore God is not ashamed to be called their God, for he has prepared for them a city.

–HEBREWS 11:14–16

We began these pages with images of home or running away from it, and the perspective that distance affords. Often the journey, however long and detoured, lands us in the same location we started from. But it looks different now, and should. Home hasn't changed, any more than the Church changes into something it never was before; but we have changed.

Hence these reflections are a look out the kitchen window. Their goal is only to explore what is already in our own backyards (or basements or attics, for that matter) and to consider whether we might want to bring these persons and events back inside to see them afresh, reconnect and interact with them, claiming them once more as our family and inheritance. They have not grown old, and this is how they differ from nostalgia: We're not dusting off the tattered and faded past, but drinking again from an ever-fresh, ever-flowing stream.

I hope that the several points chosen for meditation will inspire further reflection on the many topics left out—omitted not because secondary or unimportant, but because our Faith is so rich and multi-faceted that not everything can be said, or needs to be said, in a single book. If you wish, for example, to reflect more on the Blessed Trinity or on the several sacraments not covered here, now is the time to set out on your return journey home, and savor your own discoveries. God will reward the effort.

I have deliberately avoided the catechetical or apologetic approach, not because accuracy of doctrine doesn't matter, but because plenty of fine Catholic resources already exist in print or online forms that answer basic questions about biblical and Church teaching. Here, our program has been to show that once you know the truth there remains the work of contemplating the truth, letting it sink in, letting it change you. Very many of our Lord's contemporaries knew the Scriptures backwards and forwards, especially the scholars of the law, yet relatively few allowed the known truth to come alive before them in the person of the incarnate Word.

In light of this, I offer a concluding consideration, touching the outbound leg of many people's sojourn into the world, before they find out the world isn't all it's cracked up to be and the thought of turning back starts looking good. How someone reverses direction after breakneck pursuit of the world's promises needs some looking at. And let's remember that by "the world" we mean the fallen world, the world that doesn't look or get beyond itself, the world that Scripture soberly judges as having little to offer except "the lust of the flesh and the lust of the eyes and the pride of life" (1 Jn 2:16). It's also worth emphasizing here that one who ventures into worldliness need not ever leave the comfort of home. We're talking here mainly about the drifting of mind and heart.

Many people leave the Church behind because they find her irrelevant, anachronistic, or totally lacking in credibility. At her worst, she might be all these and more. But if she is in such a sorry state that leaving her seems like the thing to do, it is because her members have stopped thinking about, praying over, and applying such things as are in this book, and so are not credible as believers in a revelation that comes from God and leads right back to him. Or if the problem is irrelevance, it is often because both clergy and the faithful have ceased to challenge and enlighten the world with the splendor of truth. And if anachronistic, it is not because Christians are living in the Middle Ages, but in, say, the 1970s—that is, stuck on the architectural, artistic, and liturgical fads and fashions of a commonly-regarded decade of bad taste rather than maintaining the richness of the perennial faith "once for all delivered to the saints" (Jude 1:3).

The take-away is, as has often been observed (even by the likes of Mahatma Gandhi): Christians are often at fault for the failure of

Christianity and for driving others away from it. But Christians are also responsible for its success, and when it succeeds it is nothing less than glorious. Nothing is more attractive than holiness, as embodied especially in people, because Jesus wants his own personal and divine beauty to radiate through human faces and gestures more than anywhere else. Some beautiful lines from the Jesuit poet Gerard Manley Hopkins distill the point:

…for Christ plays in ten thousand places,
Lovely in limbs, and lovely in eyes not his
To the Father through the features of men's faces.[1]

But to disfigure the beauty of Christ, to mar the dignity of the Church, often repels those seeking the truth, if it doesn't create despair of ever finding it. It's not that Christianity is in any way defective; it is the definitive revelation of Jesus Christ for the salvation of all who will believe in it. But if we return to St. John Paul II's warning in the opening pages, we will recall that Christians who don't pray and revisit the Gospel frequently are in danger of losing their faith and causing others to be lost as well. Jesus demands living witnesses. Those begging off to go and bury their dead are themselves as good as dead when the Gospel of life is at stake (See: Mt 8:19–22).

But before we follow the road out of town, it's only fair to say that the world offers no better alternative to the Christian creed. It's the same old temptations, the same old sins, that have never succeeded

1   Gerard Manley Hopkins, "As Kingfishers Catch Fire," in *The Major Works*, ed. Catherine Phillips (New York: Oxford University Press, 2002), p. 129.

in producing lasting peace, happiness, joy, or fulfillment in anyone. Although it does a clever forgery of them all, the counterfeit eventually shows its bankruptcy—its inability to pay human debts: debts of conscience, of desire, and of love, which only God can pay.

Although trying to dissuade a runaway is typically pointless, there is great peace in knowing that God is closely tracking each and every fugitive, reaching them as only he can, through means that would likely shock them if they knew what he was up to. No one can outrun the Lord. He can use even the swiftness of the fugitive's flight, in boomerang fashion, as a gathering impetus for their eventual return. In these final paragraphs, I will once again enlist St. John Henry Newman for insight into how God accomplishes this seemingly impossible work of retrieval.

When prodigal children book passage for a far country, the last thing they want is a reminder about the likeliness of a U-turn. No ticket kiosk offering roundtrip fare will likely greet them at the border, and that is just as well. When worldly expectations are great and hopes high, the runaway can't get into the mix of the world fast enough.

Often unnoticed, if not ignored, is the long procession of disillusioned and broken people on the return journey. Ironically, the world is often the cause of its own depopulation. Yet in the providence of him who numbers the hairs on our heads, there is no irony. The bitterness that inevitably follows worldly indulgence is a symptom of the deeper sickness that Jesus came to heal. The deceptive goods themselves that people run after can serve as God's unsuspected means of returning them to himself.

The lost are found in this way, Newman explains, "by finding disappointment and suffering from that which they had hoped would bring them good."[2]

> [T]hey learn to love God and prize heaven, not by baptismal grace, but by trial of the world; they seek the world, and they are driven by the world back again to God. The world is blessed to them, in God's good providence, as an instrument of His grace transmuted from evil to good, as if a second sacrament, doing over again what was done in infancy, and then undone.[3]

A soul's turning point need not involve the obvious drama of the parable of the prodigal son. If we assume that every unconverted person is feverish or grasping in his pursuit of worldly happiness, we take the extreme for the norm, and bypass more modest self-application. In reality, to be worldly is simply to believe that the (admittedly) unreliable happiness this world offers is the only happiness worth pursuing, and to act practically and regularly on that belief. No attempt at transcendence is seriously embarked on. Happiness comes from the world and remains in it without ever getting beyond it.

This creates a deeper problem in us that Newman identifies as an incurable loneliness. More than separating someone from his or her hometown, or even homeland, the world's unfulfilled and unfulfillable

2   Newman, "The Church, a Home for the Lonely," p. 186.
3   Newman.

promises of happiness end up separating a person not only from God but also from the world itself. The world is self-alienating.

For a season, buying into the world's promises of happiness seems the best use of time, money, effort, and love. But eventually the repetition of pleasures and amusements emerges for what it always was: a surface distraction against inner loneliness, aggravated by the very diversions themselves.

Poet Matthew Arnold, a contemporary and admirer of Newman, wistfully noted this discrepancy in his classic poem "Dover Beach." The world, seeming to provide for every need, cannot give what matters most:

> ...for the world, which seems
> To lie before us like a land of dreams,
> So various, so beautiful, so new,
> Hath really neither joy, nor love, nor light,
> Nor certitude, nor peace, nor help for pain...[4]

Although Arnold's poem leaves largely unidentified where these good things may be found, Newman points the way to a wholly unique, God-given "shelter, refuge, rest, home or sanctuary from the outward world,"[5] locating our safe haven in

> the Church of God, which is our true home of God's providing,

4 Matthew Arnold, "Dover Beach," in *Poetical Works of Matthew Arnold* (London: Macmillan & Co., 1892), pp. 226–7.

5 Newman, "The Church a Home for the Lonely," p. 187.

His own heavenly court, where He dwells with Saints and Angels, into which He introduces us by a new birth, and in which we forget the outward world and its many troubles.[6]

Religious or not, world-weariness besets everyone born into the world. People naturally look around for solutions, or remedies, even if they remain stop-gap measures. Where people end up remains uncertain. Yet land somewhere they must, because even though "they will not accept God's remedy, yet they confess that a remedy is needed, and have recourse to what they think will prove such."[7]

Enter the Gospel. God walks the earth in Christ, entering the lives of people surviving but deteriorating, in need of living water, living bread, the fresh air of the Spirit. Time and again Jesus seeks out those who have hit bottom or who are outwardly well off, but misguided. From the Samaritan woman to the rich young man, the Lord encounters people trying to make their home in this world as best they can but who need to be saved, not only from the world, but more importantly *from themselves*.

The Gospels show Jesus treating people in just this way: as needing to be called, found, caught, brought back, and protected. He compares disciples to netted fish, birds protected in the branches of a large, shady tree, and to the sheep of a guarded fold. He couldn't be clearer: Fallen people are prone to stray and need to be guided, protected, even rescued often—and then brought home.

6   Newman, p. 190.

7   Newman.

One way or another, to belong to Christ is to live in a sheepfold, a net; it is to rest in the shade of a great tree; it is to be found and rejoiced over by your rescuer. In all cases, to be saved is to belong to Christ as his treasured possession and to live in union with others likewise caught, called in, guarded, found and brought back. And this is the Church of God.

If the Prodigal Son may be taken as the paradigm for all conversions, Newman sees the world itself as the unwitting cause of numerous returns from the distant country of dissipation. It ends up repelling those most prepared to embrace its values and standards. But the itinerary of famous gospel wanderers—a straying sheep, the Prodigal Son, the Samaritan woman—should not be misunderstood. Separation from the Lord is measured not primarily by traveling distance, but by an isolation of the heart.

And for this loneliness to set in, all that is needed is for love, hope, and faith to be misplaced. To force the world to be our lasting home, our land of dreams, and to pigeonhole ourselves as its tenants, is to misread entirely the message written into creation. The world is neither a paradise nor a prison, but the training ground for love and freedom. The disappointments encountered should make us recalculate our prospects for earthly happiness in a salutary way. They can set the heart free from dependence on the world, attachment to its attractions, so that we can enter into the company and communion of God and his saints.

These are inspiring thoughts for the solitary, the dejected, the harassed, the defamed, or the despised Christian; and they belong to him, if by act and deed he unites in that Communion which he professes. He joins the Church of God, not merely who speaks about it, or who defends it, or who contemplates it, but who loves it.[8]

And it is perhaps most especially in the absence of this love, or when confronted with its counterfeit, that the heart is stirred to desire its authentic and lasting expression in the Church of God, love's genuine home. That Church is Scripture's "holy city, [the] New Jerusalem, coming down out of heaven from God, prepared as a bride adorned for her husband" (Rev 21:2). And the promise of this bride-city guarantees nothing less than the mutual, eternal abiding of God with his people.

It is no accident that the Bible both begins and ends with home. Adam and Eve are given a paradise in which to live, wherein they may commune freely and intimately with the Lord. After their fall and banishment, the long and lonely hunger of their children is for reinstatement in that peaceful and secure dwelling with their Creator, their divine Lover and Bridegroom. It is this that the last page of Scripture promises, and where the written word of God ends, and so will we:

> "Behold, the dwelling of God is with men. He will dwell with them, and they shall be his people, and God himself

---

8   John Henry Newman, "The Communion of Saints," in *Parochial and Plain Sermons*, vol. 4, pp. 183–4.

will be with them; he will wipe away every tear from their eyes, and death shall be no more, neither shall there be mourning nor crying nor pain any more, for the former things have passed away."

And he who sat upon the throne said, "Behold, I make all things new." Also he said, "Write this, for these words are trustworthy and true." And he said to me, "It is done! I am the Alpha and the Omega, the beginning and the end. To the thirsty I will give water without price from the fountain of the water of life. He who conquers shall have this heritage, and I will be his God and he shall be my son" (Rev 21:3–7).